Adapting Quilt Patterns to Polymer Clay

Judith Skinner & Sarajane Helm

Photographs by Sarajane Helm, graphics by Judith Skinner except as noted.
Prepared with Sun Microsystem Open Office suite and Adobe Photoshop.

First published and printed in paperback in the United States of America
November 2006 by PolyMarket Press

ISBN 978-0-9800312-1

For more information about our books and the authors and artists
who create them, please visit our website:

PolyMarketPress.com

This book is dedicated to:

The women who brought us all the lovely quilt patterns through the years.

Each new block was a gift that lived past many generations.

*Every quilt has a background composed of the memories, the love
and the labor which went into its creation.*

*For all those unsung women who stitched together their stories along with
bits and pieces of cotton, silk and wool into something of service and beauty,
we are grateful and warmed.*

We also thank:

Our polymer clay sisters at Pingree and Shrinemont.

Sarajane's husband Bryan, sons Ian and Andy,
mother Mary, and sister Kelly
for their love and years of cooperation.

Judith's sister Chris Pearson and family who are always
available with support and encouragement.

Margie Drake for her warmth and cooperation.

Mary Rosello who is always there to care for Judith's animal
kingdom during her many absences, and Annie, Jackson,
Jessica, Callie and Hobbes who tolerate her many absences.

Judith's fellow artists in the Arts Prescott and Jerome
Cooperative Galleries for inspiration and incentive.

Donna Kato and Marie Segal for the years of effort they have
each given to improving the world of polymer clay.

Lindly Haunani and Leigh Ross who went
above and beyond the call.

All of the artists who contributed their fabulous work to be
seen in the gallery and in "Pieces".

The polymer clay community for decades of
sharing and enthusiasm.

The past twenty years have been an extremely exciting time for artists using polymer clay as an expressive art medium. As the techniques, tools and clays have evolved, so have the artistic approaches evolved. Many techniques have been adapted from other mediums with great success; including metal smithing, basket making and ceramics.

Quilting, with its rich traditions of innovation, collaboration and improvisation is especially conducive for adaptation to use with polymer clay. It is possible to cane quilt blocks in polymer clay and then combine them in dozens of different orientations. Sheets of clay can be designed to be used as "fabric" to collage together into three dimensional quilts of clay. Mosaic pieces can be cut into squares, triangles and diamonds and then recombined into fascinating, changeable patterns. Blocks can be traded, morphed or recombined with the work of others. The possibilities are seemingly endless.

Last spring Sarajane came up with the brilliant idea to make a miniature quilt shop to be used in this book and document its construction on her web site. I volunteered (I must admit with some reluctance) to take the bolt templates and instructions to a polymer clay retreat. I was absolutely amazed, delighted and inspired by the response of the artists.

The participants at this retreat rose to the challenge by making over 100 bolts of fabric, nearly six pounds, for the miniature quilt shop. The colorways ranged from bright neons to subdued fall shades. The techniques used included surface textures, caning, mokume gane and silk screened patterns. Each fabric was a unique expression of the contributing artist's personality. As the collection continued to amass, it inspired others to participate and we set up a display table. The temptation to rearrange and recombine the arrangement of the bolts of fabric was hard to resist. This project was an excellent example of the synergy of collaborative creation, where the joyful whole becomes much more than the individual pieces.

This past summer I watched over a period of days as Judith developed and made the step outs for one of the quilt patterns in this book. Her attention to detail, precision and conceptualization of the pattern belies her genius when it comes to working with polymer clay. And in case you are wondering, Judith Skinner is the inventor of the Skinner blend, which is one most useful ways to create polymer clay blends.

The time is succulently ripe for a book dedicated to Adapting Quilt Patterns to Polymer Clay. Both Sarajane and Judith bring years of experience, enthusiasm and expertise to this book.

I look forward with great anticipation to seeing the wonderful things that will be inspired by this book. Undoubtedly there will be gallery exhibits, on-line swaps, polymer quilting bees and technical innovations inspired by this book.

Remember to have fun and play with the clay!

Lindly Haunani

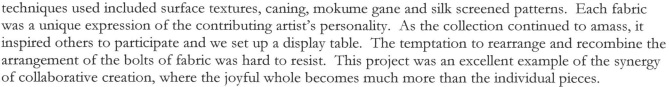

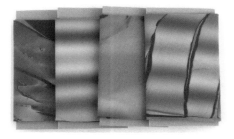
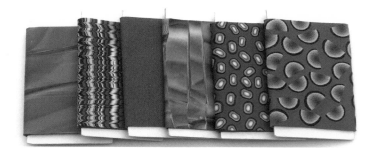

4

Table of Contents

1. Properties of Polymer Clay 7

2. Tools 11

3. Color 16

4. Elements of Caning 21

5. Quilt Block Patterns 24

   ○ Amish Bars 26

   ○ Amish Center Diamond 30

   ○ Nine-Patch 36

   ○ Nine-Patch Variation 42

   ○ Log Cabin 50

   ○ Lone Star 58

   ○ Sunshine and Shadow 64

   ○ Drunkard's Path 70

   ○ Tumbling Blocks 74

6. Print Design Variations 78

7. Surface Applications 84

   ○ Mosaics, Tiles and Textures 88

   ○ Hawaiian Appliqué 90

8. "Pieces" - The Miniature Textile Shoppe 92

9. Gallery 98

10. Artist Information 108

11. Sources 112

12. References 115

13. Glossary 118

"Pieces" – The Miniature Textile Shoppe

1. Properties of Polymer Clay

The world of textile design with its infinite variations in color and pattern would seem to offer enough choices to astound and gratify anyone seeking the sensory pleasures of the eye and hand. And yet, to a quilter that is only a starting point. This very particular genre of artist yearns to marry parts together; to arrange, juxtapose and recombine blocks using small pieces of carefully chosen textiles creating new images in fabric. Color, tonal range, shape and precision of placement are all vital to creating a beautiful quilt top.

Quilters transform small bits of cloth into warm coverlets and gorgeous works of art that are passed along for generations.

Taking these abilities into the world of polymer clay requires a little practical information, a few tools, and some practice. The same choices in color, texture and pattern pertain to polymer clay, especially when adapting quilt designs. Many of the skills and some of the tools used in quilting translate readily to polymer clay.

Polymer clay is a synthetic modeling material, not an earth clay. It is formulated from polyvinyl chloride (PVC), dyes and pigments and plasticizer. To be 'plastic' is to be capable of change, malleable, able to be formed. These terms certainly describe polymer clay. It can be used to mimic everything from wood, stone, shell and bone to paper and fabric. Artists and designers from many different areas have embraced its use in doll-making, miniatures, jewelry, and two- and three-dimensional art. The medium is almost as unlimited in its potential as imagination itself.

Brands and Forms of Polymer Clays

Polymer clay is available from many craft stores and from polymer clay Internet sites. The working properties vary between brands and become a personal choice requiring experimentation. The most common clays used in making canes are FIMO Classic™, Kato Polyclay™ and Sculpey Premo!™. Within each of these brands there are opaque colors, translucent clays and pearlized colors containing fine mica powders.

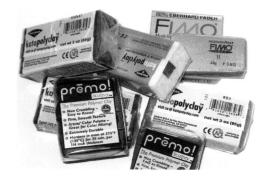

Polymer clay is also available in a liquid form useful for bonding raw to finished clay. Liquid polymer clay can also be used to transfer many images. Sculpey Diluent™ is a liquid plasticizer (not a polymer clay) which can be mixed into any of the polymer clays to soften old or hard clays.

There are many other clays which have characteristics that are not appropriate for precision caning but have other useful applications including Sculpey III™, FimoSoft™, Cernit™, Modello™ and Dukit™.

Conditioning Polymer Clay

All polymer clays must be conditioned before using them in any project, even the clays that are already quite soft. Conditioning makes the clay more malleable and softer; it also aligns the molecules and makes it stronger. Without proper conditioning, cured pieces will be fragile and brittle.

To condition polymer clay by hand, slice and chop the clay into small pieces. Knead and roll the clay into a snake shape, stretch it out, fold it over several times and roll it back into a snake. Do this at least ten times.

Conditioning polymer clay with a pasta machine simplifies and speeds up the process. Cut clay into approximately ¼" thick slices. Roll the slices through the pasta machine on the thickest setting. Stack a couple of slices together and roll them through together. Stack these, turn them sideways and roll them through again. Repeating this process with several slices will form a sheet of clay. Fold the sheet in half, roll this through the pasta machine inserting the folded edge first. Do this 20 to 25 times.

One way to know how long it takes to condition polymer clay is to mix colors. Do the conditioning process with pieces of two or more colors. When the colors are fully mixed into a solid color, the clay is fully conditioned. Inversely, it is not necessary to condition clay before mixing colors or before doing a 'Skinner Blend'. The mixing/blending process fully conditions polymer clay.

If your polymer clay is too soft for caning, it can be made more workable by 'wicking' or 'leaching' excess plasticizer from the clay. Roll the clay into sheets and place between two pieces of newsprint or copier paper. Leave the sheets between the paper for an hour or two. You must be able to fold the clay without any cracking along the fold. Leigh Ross recommends putting sheets of clay between paper, sitting on it for 5-10 minutes to be sure it is not leached too much. Removing too much plasticizer can weaken the clay. For best long term results, allow soft clays to stay packaged, in a cool dry place to 'age'. Several months later the clay will be firmer without the loss of strength leaching can introduce.

Storing Polymer Clay

Store polymer clay in a cool area, out of direct sunlight. As it will begin to cure at about 120°F, do not leave polymer clay in a vehicle on a hot day. If possible, order clay in bulk during cool months to avoid shipping raw clay in high temperatures.

To eliminate dust and pet hairs from contaminating your polymer clay surfaces, use plastic wrap to cover work in progress and raw clay if you need to leave it. Use plastic wrap or sandwich bags to store cane lengths and unpackaged raw clay. Check your plastic wraps. Over time some plastic wraps will interact with polymer clay. We use Saran™ with Cling as we know it does not interact. Also, as polymer clay will interact with some hard plastics, do not store raw clay in plastic containers without first wrapping the clay.

When starting a major project we like to roll the clay into sheets about 6" long on the thickest pasta machine setting, then place each sheet on a Hefty™ sandwich (the ones without flaps or ziplocks) and stack the sheets ready for use. Deli-style parchment paper also works well between the sheets of clay as it will not leach the plasticizers.

Add-Ins

Many art supplies can be added to polymer clay to create some very beautiful effects. Most of them can be used on the surface or worked into the clay. Pigments and powders can be applied to the surface of textured clay to highlight the design. Especially effective are Pearl-Ex™ Powders containing powdered mica. They are available in a wide range of metallic and reflective colors. When worked into the clay, the powder disperses at first in a localized swirl. Then it moves throughout the entire mass as you continue to work the clay. The more translucent the clay, the more powders and other inclusions seem to float. Opalescent effects can be seen, especially when translucent clays are finished to a high sheen.

Glitter, metal leaf, confetti and fibers can also be used on the surface or mixed into polymer clays. Embossing powders, alcohol dyes and stamp ink in both dye and pigment forms create many interesting effects. These inclusions are all more apparent with translucent clays. Finding new and different supplies to add to polymer clay is another opportunity for experimentation.

When working with fine powders wearing a dust mask is highly recommended, as is working in a draft-free area.

Oven Curing

All polymer clays are cured by heat, usually between 250°F and 300°F for 30 minutes for small projects. Exact temperatures and baking times are printed on the clay packaging. Pieces can be baked in a home oven, a large toaster oven or a convection oven, but never a microwave oven. Many polymer clay artists have a toaster or small convection oven dedicated to polymer clay. When using their home oven for larger projects, many artists will tent their baking trays with foils or use a closed roasting pan when using their home oven. Never heat food and clay in the same oven at the same time.

The most important thing about safely baking polymer clays is **not to overheat** the clay. With most clays scorching will begin at temperatures just over 300°F. Toxic fumes can occur at 390°F. Conversely, baking at temperatures that are too low will not fully cure the clays and pieces will become crumbly over time and break.

Watch for darkening or melting indicating the oven temperature is too high. As many oven thermostats are off by several degrees, use a free-standing oven thermometer and test various areas in your oven. Some corners can be hot spots. Small toaster ovens can burn clays near the heating coils when other areas in the oven may not be hot enough to fully cure polymer clay. Convection and some electric ovens will spike while preheating.

The fumes are not toxic unless the clay is burning. Keep your oven in a well-ventilated area. If you find the odor of curing clay noticeable or even unpleasant, put your oven in an isolated area. Placing the oven in a cold or drafty area may cause temperature fluctuations so watch your thermometer.

As we both are constantly baking polymer clay, we have dedicated convection/toaster ovens — Sarajane's in her laundry room, Judith's on a kitchen counter. Both are near outside doors.

Finishing Polymer Clay Pieces

Polymer clay can be sanded and buffed after baking. This will smooth the surface and ultimately adds a sheen to the finish. Sanding should be done in water containing a few drops of dishwashing detergent using increasingly finer grit wet-or-dry sandpapers. Buffing can be done by hand with a rough textured cloth like denim or using a buffing wheel. Translucent clays can be made almost transparent with sanding and buffing. If dry sanding, use care and a dust mask. When using power buffing tools, wear protective eyewear and keep long hair and shirt sleeves away from the wheel. See *Chapter 2 – Tools* for details.

As the projects shown in this book are intended to imitate fabric with a matte surface, they required little if any finishing after curing. Care was taken when cutting and forming the pieces to avoid fingerprints and other surface imperfections. Smoothing cane slices under plastic wrap is usually enough to eliminate these steps.

When powders or foils are used in surface applications, a protective coating can be added to the cured clay. Brushing a thin coating of a liquid clay on the surface of a cured piece and baking again is one solution. Other protective coatings are available. Use only water-based products with polymer clay as coatings containing solvents will react with clay over time making it tacky.

Many artists use Rust-Oleum Varathane™, a water based interior polyurethane. The spray version of this product is compatible with polymer clay; though other aerosol finishes may later become sticky. A high gloss finish can also be formed with Future™, an acrylic floor polish. There are finishing glazes manufactured specifically for polymer clay in both Fimo™ and Sculpey™ formulations. These protective coatings can be applied or blotted with a make-up sponge for a matte finish.

Tips and Precautions

Polymer clays are certified as a non-toxic art material. However, it is always wise to use common sense and stay on the side of caution. Polymer clays should not be used for items that come in direct contact with foods or liquids. Both raw and cured clay can interact with perfume oils, hair spray and some lotions. Pieces made with polymer clay should not be heated to high temperatures or come in contact with flame.

When a kitchen tool is used with polymer clay, do not return it to the kitchen. Baking trays should not be used for food after baking polymer clay on them. Dedicate these tools to your artwork and get new ones for the kitchen.

Wash your hands before and after working with polymer clays or with any of the powders, inks, finishes and pigments you may use with them. Some artists wear latex or nitrile gloves to limit skin contact and to avoid fingerprints on the clay. One good way to remove polymer clay residue from your hands and tools is with baby wipes. It is also a very good idea to regularly use a lotion on your hands as dry skin and rough spots make smoothing your clay pieces more difficult.

Nancy Osbahr

2. Tools

Polymer clay artists can make use of an amazing amount of stuff. Many kitchen tools and office supplies find their way into the studio; many other art and craft supplies will have a new use. When first experimenting with polymer clay the only must-haves are a **sharp** blade, a way to roll out even sheets of clay and an oven. For the projects in this book, a pasta machine and measuring aids can be included in the list of must-haves.

Work Surfaces

Your work surface should be smooth, nonporous and preferably portable. Marble, ceramic or acrylic tiles, file folders and even large index cards can be used on your table top for preparing clay. In general, when you want your project to move around easily on your work surface, use paper; when you want it to stay in place, use an acrylic sheet or tile. One lovely work surface borrowed from quilters is a rotary cutting mat with a grid. Do not work directly on a wooden table top as the clay will interact with many wood finishes.

Cutting Tools

Blades and knives are useful for slicing clay in quantity and also for making thin, even slices of canes once they are formed. A craft or X-acto™ knife is excellent for cutting elements out of flat sheets, but a long flat blade is best for cane slicing. A shorter, sturdier blade gives you better control when slicing a cane. There are many available now in craft stores or from on-line suppliers with varying degrees of flexibility for making curves or very straight cuts. There are even wavy blades! A quick brush of cornstarch on your blade helps cut down on dragging.

There are also several cane slicers on the market. Hold your blade at an angle when using any of them. A good old-style cheese paring knife with no serration on the blade is good for sliding underneath work to separate it cleanly when needed, but often not sharp enough for cane slicing. Our recent favorite new tool is a WUSTHOF™ Cheese Knife – a good investment if you do a lot of polymer clay. This sturdy blade measures five inches in length and is very comfortable to use when slicing slabs of clay for conditioning and when making long unwavering cuts. Just as with fabric quilting, the right cutting tools are crucial. See *Chapter 11 – Sources* for suppliers.

Clay Rollers

"Roll a sheet of polymer clay ... " are often the first words in a set of polymer clay project guidelines. This can be done with an acrylic rod, with a brayer or even with a rolling pin. However, a pasta machine is the fastest and easiest way to roll even sheets of clay at consistent thicknesses. Atlas™ pasta machines have set the standard for polymer clay and are readily available. Atlas is a well-built, sturdy machine that can last for years. It can even be *carefully* disassembled for cleaning.

You can attach an electric motor to most pasta machines which makes conditioning and color mixing faster and more consistent. Having two hands free to manipulate large sheets of clay is convenient.

Brayers and rollers are ideal for smoothing seams and compressing canes after they are assembled and are nice to include in your polymer clay tool collection.

Atlas thickness settings:

#1 – 1/8"
#2 – 3/32"
#3 – 1/16" (half #1)
#4 – 1/20"
#5 – 1/24"
#6 – 1/32" (half #3)
#7 – card stock thickness

(#8 and #9 if available, are very thin)

Pasta machines often come with a noodle cutter attachment. This piece is heavy and many artists remove it for convenience. However, do not lose track of it because it is very useful for cutting even strips of clay. There are two sizes meant for spaghetti and fettuccine.

We often make pieces to be used in edging or mosaics by baking thin sheets of clay, then running the warm cured sheets through the cutters. Small square tiles for mosaics can be easily formed by cutting the strips using sharp scissors or a rotary cutter.

Measuring Aids

Graph paper, rulers, cutting guides and templates all make precise pieces easier to achieve.

Create your own templates and patterns for shapes you cut often using matte board or acrylic sheets meant for making stencils.

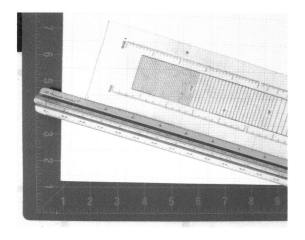

Extruders

An extruder designed for polymer clay is a wonderful tool for creating cane elements that are sized and shaped just right and allow for fitted and repeated cane elements. There is a wide range in the size, price and ease of use in the models available on the market today. Each has its good qualities, and finding the one that works best for your needs might take some trials. There are also devices available to make the plunger action of the Kemper Gun easier on the hands.

In our preparations for the making the canes in this book we used extruders made by PolyPress, Polymer Clay Express and Kemper. In addition to the standard discs (the shaped dies) that come with some of those tools, there are discs from Polymer Clay Express and Jenny Patterson of Quilted in Clay that are specifically shaped with quilt block patterns in mind. Darlin' Designer Discs also have many interesting shapes and sets available, but note that they need to be cleaned after use to avoid long term interaction. See *Chapter 11 — Sources* for suppliers.

Polymer Clay Express Extruder with small discs

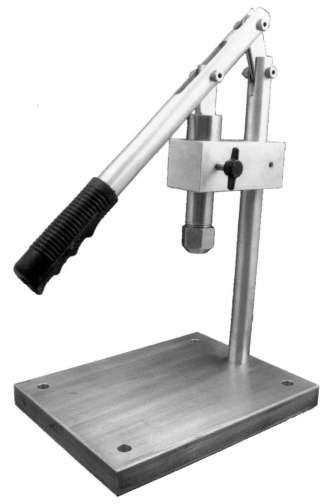

Kemper Gun & discs, Darlin' Discs and Quilted In Clay dies

PolyPress Extruder

Texturing and Stamping

Texture sheets, rubber stamps, coarse sandpapers, lace and many other items can be used to texture and add visual interest to polymer clay. Acrylic sheets made by Shadex™ have many designs available and the positive and negative side are each a different effect. Inks or pearlized powders can be added to the raised surfaces or acrylic paints and stains can be used to fill the depressed areas.

When using stamps or texture sheets, a release agent is helpful. Some use talcum powder or cornstarch brushed on lightly or applied with a ponce bag. We find that a light spritz of water from a spray bottle works well, particularly with Premo!™ and Kato Polyclay™. Mist the surface of the stamp or sheet and then press onto the sheet of clay. For best results roll the clay and texture piece together through the pasta machine. This works with unmounted rubber stamps, texture sheets or sandpaper cut to size.

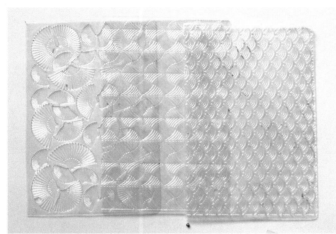

Shadex Texture Sheets

Some restrictions apply to the use of rubber stamps for profit. Only companies with an 'angel policy' allow limited commercial use.

You can also have your own stamps made. Use your own designs or those that are copyright free and available to artists in the Dover Pictorial Archive and clip art sources, and you can use the resulting stamps as freely as you like.

When ordering stamps from Ready Stamps™ (a sheltered workshop division of Cerebral Palsy Association), you can also get the matrix tray. This is a mold used in forming the stamps and it is most useful with polymer clay!

See *Chapter 11 – Sources* for suppliers.

Ready Stamp rubber stamps and matrix sets

Baking Surfaces

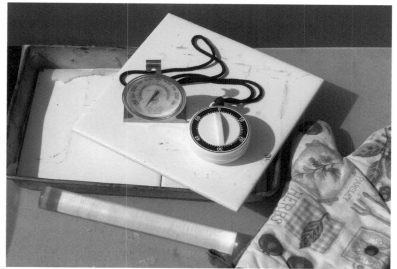
Baking tools and an acrylic rod roller

Use baking pans that are dedicated to polymer clay.

Ceramic tiles, polyester fiber-fill, paper and felt squares can be used to line pans for better temperature control and to help support any curved or bent pieces while baking.

Puffs of fiber-fill will not burn, but can leave stray fibers in the clay. Paper and felt keep the back of the piece from becoming shiny.

Always use a thermometer and timer to help keep to baking times and temperatures.

Sanding and Buffing

Drywall mesh can be used for texture or to sand edges down quickly. Emory boards are easy to use to smooth edges of small pieces.

From coarse to ultra smooth, sandpaper can be used to impart texture, or to remove fingerprints and minor imperfections. Use very coarse wet-dry paper and spray lightly with water before putting it through the pasta machine with a sheet of clay for texture, or use it under the clay piece as you work to impart a texture to the back.

Prepare baked items for buffing by using successively finer grits, ending with 1000 grit automotive grade paper. Then buff with a soft cloth or a muslin buffing wheel.

When using a power buffer, take care not to scorch the clay by holding it too long in one spot. Wear good eye protection, as small items can be flung by the wheel.

3. Color

Working with colors is one of the most exciting and challenging experiences you can have with polymer clay. Choosing just the right color scheme for a project can seem to be a daunting task. The basic principles of color theory can make this process less accidental and a little more deliberate.

Lindly Haunani and Margaret Maggio are the polymer clay color gurus. Their passion for color has been shared with polymer clay artists around the world. Attending a workshop on color with these two artists is the best way to get a real understanding of color and its importance in polymer clay.

The Color Wheel

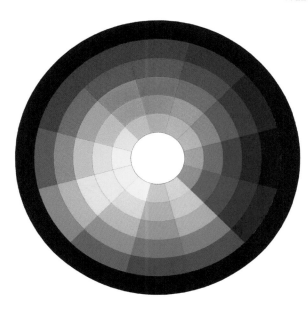

The color wheel is a simple way to represent the color spectrum. The **Primary** colors red, blue and yellow cannot be made from any other colors. All other colors in the color wheel can be mixed from these three colors.

Secondary colors are mixed with equal parts of the primary colors. Red and blue make violet, blue and yellow make green, yellow and red make orange. **Tertiary** colors are mixed with equal parts of primary and secondary colors. For example, red and orange make red-orange.

Hue is simply the name used for any color mixed from the primary colors. Red, yellow-green and blue-violet are hues.

Value describes the darkness or lightness of a specific hue mixed with black or white. Adding black to a hue gives a darker **Shade**; adding white to a hue gives a lighter **Tint.**

This color wheel has primary, secondary and tertiary **Hues** arranged in order in the middle ring. The inner two rings are **Tints** where the hues have been mixed with different amounts of white. The outer two rings are **Shades** where the hues have been mixed with different amounts of black.

Saturation and **Intensity** are other words used to describe **Value**. Pure **Hues** are fully saturated; they are at their highest intensity.

Color Schemes and Color Harmonies

Monochromatic means using one color throughout, utilizing various tints and shades.

Complimentary colors are opposites on the color wheel such as red and green or blue and orange. Varying tints and shades can give a dramatic effect.

Analogous colors neighbor each other on the color wheel. **Warm** colors appear on the left side (reds, oranges, yellows) while **Cool** colors are on the right side (blues and violets).

Triadic colors are three hues that are an equal distance apart on the color wheel such as red, yellow and blue or yellow-green, red-orange and blue-violet.

Many books and Internet websites explore the world of color in great detail. A few of these are listed in *Chapter 12 - References.*

Mixing Colors

In theory, mixing colors in polymer clay is like mixing colors in paint. However, as polymer clay is a solid, it is actually easier to measure proportions and produce the same results each time. An easy way to test color mixes is to roll sheets of the starting colors, cut out little pieces of the same sizes using a small cutter and mix the pieces. When experimenting with color mixes, keep track of the proportions, bake the results and start a sample board or journal.

Using colors straight from the package will work with many of the patterns illustrated in this book. Many quilt patterns are done in bright, simple colors. Even these colors can be altered slightly for interesting effects. As some colors in some clays appear to darken slightly when baked, adding a small amount of white will lessen the darkening. Adding a small amount of black will tone down the intensity of a color to mimic antique or Civil War era dye tones. For really bright colors, try adding small amounts of fluorescent colors to your mixes.

Quilt Block Pattern Colors

The colors used in the illustrations for the Quilt Block patterns are intended to present possible color combinations and stimulate color experiments. Some of them represent colors straight from the package. Some have lights (tints) with the addition of white or off-white and darks (shades) with the addition of black or dark brown.

All of the patterns have color variations shown in the introductory photograph and detailed illustrations following the step-by-step guidelines. Most of the variations also show a black, white and red combination for a more contemporary option.

Amish Bars and Amish Center Diamond

The primary and secondary hues represent the brilliant colors often seen in Amish Quilts. These can be lightened with an ecru or champagne color for subtle yet traditional Amish colors.

Nine-Patch

The single Nine-Patch block is shown in a simple monochromatic brown, ecru, and white. The double Nine-Patch is livened up with the addition of teal or blue-green. The full Nine-Patch quilt pattern blends the white and teal colors creating a halo effect around the center.

Nine-Patch Variation

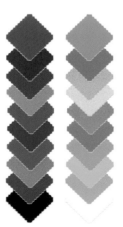

This selection of colors might represent a quilter's fabric stash. The lighter values are a mix of the original colors with an equal amount of white. Black is used for contrast. If done with a dark brown contrast, the colors could be lightened with ecru or off-white.

Log Cabin

The set of blues and olive-greens used for the Log Cabin are tints and shades of a navy blue and an olive-green. As these colors are very close in value and the pattern is repeatedly reduced, a line of black visually separates the colors.

Lone Star

The color combination of browns and blues is always pleasing. It is actually a good example of a complementary color scheme, various shades and tints of blue-greens and red-oranges, complementary colors on the color wheel.

Sunshine & Shadow

Sunshine and Shadow uses three colors with a light (tint) and dark (shade) of each. The hues are split complements on the color wheel (a hue with the colors on either side of its complement), red with blue-green and yellow-green.

Drunkard's Path

Simple and dramatic, this pattern is traditionally done in blue and white.

Tumbling Blocks

This pattern shows another use of monochromatic colors. Any three colors with light, mid-range and dark values work well for this pattern. Black is used as a border accent.

The Skinner Blend

Color gradations are included in the Nine-Patch and the Lone Star patterns as simple background elements. Lone Star uses a bulls-eye cane formed from a basic two-color blend. Nine-Patch uses a log formed from the four-section blend.

Two-Color Blend

Form two rectangles in contrasting colors from sheets as wide as your pasta machine rollers (5½" standard). Cut the rectangles diagonally forming triangles.

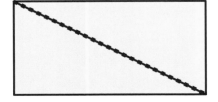

Form a rectangle using a triangle of each color.

Fold, bringing bottom edge to top. Run this through the pasta machine with the folded edge first. Repeat this 20 to 25 times.

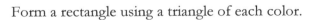

Using the Skinner Blend in a Cane

Bulls-eye Cane

Rotate the blended sheet a quarter turn. Run the sheet through the pasta machine on a thinner setting.

Roll the sheet tightly, starting with the color you want on the inside of the cane.

Four Section Blend Producing Logs

Cut four rectangles 1¾" wide, any length, in two colors. Cut the rectangles diagonally, forming triangles. Arrange the triangles.

Fold, bringing bottom edge to top. Run this through the pasta machine with the folded edge first. Repeat this 20 to 25 times.

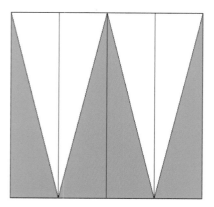

Cut this sheet, crosswise, into 2" sections. Stack the sections.

Cut this stack into four pieces lengthwise, forming logs. Stack them to form larger logs.

4. Elements of Caning

Canes and *millefiore* are terms taken from glass workers. Millefiore means *thousand flowers* in Italian and refers to a technique combining patterned and colored rods of glass to form canes, heating the canes and stretching them out. Slices of the canes are used decorate objects like beads and paper weights.

Polymer clay cane work is based on this technique with several advantages, not the least of which is the absence of flame. Wondrous variations in polymer clay cane design are possible, from the very simple to the very complex. Canes can depict geometric shapes, detailed landscapes, snowflakes, flowers and leaves, faces, lace and textiles, butterfly and angel wings, quilt blocks – even signatures!

The simple daisy cane shown above was stretched out reducing the size of the flower, cut into segments and recombined with other canes into the complex floral bouquet cane shown above right.

As a way to create repetitive patterns canes offer great graphic potential.

Cane Components

When building polymer clay canes, the beginning pieces tend to be among a limited number of shapes. Intricate images can be built using circles, triangles, rectangles and lines.

Snakes – Rolled out pieces of clay that are long, with a round diameter, like snakes. These are also known as **logs** when they are shorter and fatter. Pinch down the length of the top side of the snake to form a **teardrop** or **petal** shape.

Triangle shaped snakes are made by pinching the top of a snake and pushing down at the same time, to flatten the bottom while pointing the tops. Do this down the entire length.

Square shaped snakes are made by using the thumb and forefinger of one hand to pinch the sides and the thumb of the other to flatten the top of the snake down onto the work surface, making it into a long rectangle. Use an acrylic rod or brayer to further level the four sides of the square snake. This forms very crisp angles in the square snake.

Sheets are flat, even layers of clay, made by rolling the clay with an acrylic rod, a brayer or a pasta machine. Pasta machines give the most even layers, with seven to nine settings that range from ⅛" thick to paper thin. Sheets can be used to wrap other components. Wrapping a round snake forms a bulls-eye. The most precise way to create square cane components for quilt canes is to use a blade and cutting guide to cut strips from a stack of sheets that are as wide as the stack of sheets is thick.

Strips can be formed by flattening a snake of clay, pressing with your thumb or a roller to press it flat onto the work surface. Or a snake can be run through the pasta machine at the widest setting to form a strip. Strips can also be cut from a sheet of clay using a blade and a cutting guide. The noodle cutting attachments of the pasta machine can be used to cut two sizes of strips. Roll raw clay sheets through the cutting rollers and out come strips.

Extrusions are shaped lengths of clay made using a tool that presses soft clay through a disc with a precisely shaped opening. These precise shapes allow building detailed canes that need very little reduction.

Cut-outs are made using open backed cookie cutters or similar tools. Make a thick stack of conditioned clay between one and two inches in depth. Powder a cutter lightly on the inside walls of your cutter. Press down through the stack of clay to cut out the shape. Fill in all around the outside of the shape using a background clay in a highly contrasting color.

When building canes, it often helps to use a drawing or photograph, a piece of fabric or some other image as an inspiration or guide to a design. It is also very satisfying to just play and come up with designs that you like. Flowers do not have to be the same as their botanical counterparts! By varying colors, shapes, and direction even simple forms can be used to build up beautiful and complex patterns.

Cane Reduction

Reduction in polymer clay caning means to make a cane smaller across while stretching it in length. Reduction is an extremely important part of cane making. With canes that require very precise geometric shapes and alignment, try to build them as close to the finished size as is practical. For beginning cane builders it is best to build an initial cane that measures no more than 2" across and is at least 3" long.

Canes are reduced by carefully squeezing and compressing the cane from all sides working out from the middle of the cane to each end. As the cane is compressed, it lengthens. The proportions of a design built into the cane will not change, the image just gets smaller. There are probably as many ways to reduce a cane as there are cane builders.

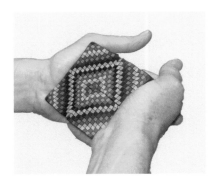

A square cane can be reduced by placing it between the heels of your hands and pressing. Rotate the cane and do this repeatedly until the cane starts to move. Then place it on a table and press down on it while slightly pulling from one end. Rotate the cane and do this repeatedly, frequently switching ends. When the cane is finally moving well, it can be pulled and smoothed with your fingertips. At the very end of the process the corners can be sharpened by using an acrylic roller.

With a round cane, start by squeezing the cane in your hand, working out from the center to the ends. Squeezing and compressing the cane in on itself takes time and patience, but causes less distortion than simply rolling a cane. Towards the end of the reduction process, however, rolling will make the cane more even and will smooth the outside. Both techniques can be used together carefully.

Slamming a large cane down on a flat surface can help wake up canes that are slow to move. As they warm, canes tend to reduce faster on the outside, so watch out for too much, too fast. Allow the cane to cool sightly if you are seeing a lot of distortion on the ends, then continue to reduce it later.

Cane Morphing

Morphing is the process of changing a component from one shape to another. It can also be done to a square cane to change the corners into the flat parts and the flat parts into corners. Gently push in on the corners of a cane up and down the length on all four sides. Begin to pinch up the area in between that used to be all the flat sides. Bring this to a peak up and down the cane on all four sides. Go back to the old corners and flatten a bit more, continue to bring the new square shape into being. Then use the acrylic roller to flatten all four new sides.

This process can also be used to change a round cane into a square cane or a square cane into a round one with interesting pattern changes occurring as part of the process.

Morphing a simple cane into a very acute triangle shape can generate a kaleidoscope or tessellation cane. Cut the new triangular cane in half, crosswise, and place two sides together forming a mirror image. Shape this back into a square or triangular cane. Reduce this new cane until you can cut 4 to 6 equal length segments from it. Place these segments together with the points in the center creating a mirror image along each segment edge. Four segments create a tessellation cane, five or more are a kaleidoscope cane.

The Most Important Elements of Cane Building

Use clays of the same consistency. They can all be hard, or soft, or in between, but if you use hard and soft clays in different areas of a cane they will not reduce evenly and will create distortion in the cane.

Choose colors that have high contrast in areas that are significantly reduced. Light and dark colors will show better together than will two colors in a medium range. Remember also that colors mixed with a white clay base will not darken during baking as much as those that have a lot of translucent or pearl in the base. Build in shading in components by using Skinner Blends or stacked sheets of clay going from light to dark.

Start your canes at least two inches long or you will not have very much finished cane. The two ends of any cane are always distorted during cane reduction. How much distortion depends on how the cane is built and how it is reduced. The inner section, past the first few inches on either end, is usually most like the image was intended to appear. The ends can have a secondary image that is part of the intended one but not complete. This distortion can sometimes be very interesting. Do not just cut the ends off and toss them in the scrap pile!

Be very careful to pack cane components tightly to avoid leaving spaces where clay will shift. Occasionally flip the cane over to check alignment.

Wrap a cane on the outside with an extra layer of clay. This will protect the image inside during reduction. The outside layer will reduce faster than the center, as it is the layer receiving the pressure and the heat from your hands, so compensate by adding a wrap. This clay will then migrate to the cane ends during reduction, rather than the outside part of your image going there. This is especially important with faces. This is also the way to keep points on stars that are on the outside of the image nice and sharp.

Allow canes to rest before reduction. If a cane gets too soft during reduction, set it aside for a while to cool down.

Reduce canes slowly and carefully. A little at a time is the correct pace for minimum distortion.

5. Quilt Block Canes

Building polymer clay canes in quilt patterns use the same processes described in *Chapter 4 – Elements of Caning*. The components are usually squares, rectangles, triangles and diamond logs. The assembly of a cane generally follows the same assembly sequence as creating a fabric quilt.

Measuring

The patterns in the following sections are filled with measurements and fractions. Quilters are familiar with precise measurements; other artists may not be as comfortable with fractions and rulers. A simple way to cut a specified width is to use eighth-inch graph paper as your cutting surface. One square is ⅛", two squares are ¼", three are ⅜" and so on. By placing a sheet of clay on the graph paper, it is not difficult to cut off an exact width strip. Use a straight-edge to cut against for straight lines.

The patterns also assume your pasta machine rolls out ⅛" thick sheets of clay. Check your machine by rolling out a sheet of clay on the thickest setting. Cut eight pieces of clay from a sheet and stack them together. If this stack does not measure really close to one inch high, you may have to compensate by rolling two sheets at a thinner setting and stacking them together to measure this very important ⅛".

Even if your machine rolls a ⅛" thick sheet, if the sheet is much thicker on one side it still might be helpful to roll two thinner sheets, flip one sheet side-to-side and stack the two sheets together. Again, find a setting that measures ⅛" thick when doubled.

If this seems like a lot of bother, just forget it, go on with the patterns and you will still create a beautiful cane. A favorite cane was made with clays of different consistencies. It did not reduce well. The slices looked like a quilt waving in the wind. It continues to be a best seller! Do what works best for you.

Black Separation Lines

Many of the patterns have a very thin sheet of black clay between the colors for a visual color separation. This allows you to use colors that are closer in value next to each other and still get a quilted look. These sheets are rolled on the thinnest setting possible on your pasta machine to actually roll a usable sheet of clay. A few inconsistencies on the sheet can be pressed out by placing a sheet of paper over the clay and smoothing.

The assembly shown here is a row of square strips that were cut from sheets of clay with a thin sheet of black on the back. The strips were rotated with the black lines between the strips. The full row is then placed on the black sheet and the black clay is cut to fit the assembled row.

Again, if this seems like a lot of bother, just forget it for now. You may want to try it on another cane as you become more familiar with the process.

Assembling Stripes

Some patterns are assembled as stripes. Cut the strips, and stack them into a cane. Place the stack on the thin black clay for the separation lines, and trim to fit.

Assembling Small Square Strips

Many of the patterns are assembled from small, square strips. These are best kept in groups of strips of the same color. They can be rotated with the black separation lines all facing the same direction.

A simple way to assemble rows of many colors is to select them and place them on an index card in the order they will be assembled. Then, using a straight-edge, slide each strip into place.

Wrapping the Finished Canes

The last step in assembling a cane is usually wrapping it with a sheet of clay representing the quilt border. For rounded corners, cut a rectangle just large enough to wrap around the cane. Place one edge close to the center of one side of the cane, wrap the rectangle around the cane, and smooth the seam.

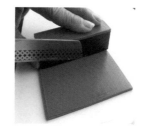

For sharp corners, place each side of the cane on a sheet of clay, and cut the clay to fit the cane. Reduce or compress the cane and smooth the seams with your fingers.

A Note About the Guidelines

In the following guidelines, the step-by-step illustrations are drawn to scale. The clay quantities are given as the size of the sheets rolled on a ⅛" setting rather than as blocks of clay because block sizes are no longer consistent between manufacturers. The quantities given are generous to provide matching clay for later use.

Amish Bars

Stark Simplicity

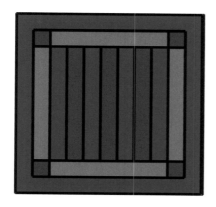

Amish Bars quilt patterns are simple vertical pieces surrounded by a border. With its inherent simplicity and straightforward design, it is reflective of patterns of the field and garden – straight furrows and wooden fences.

With a design of such stark simplicity, the colors are vitally important. The bars may be only two alternating colors, or they may be an assortment of colors. Amish Bars quilts are often pieced with a thin strip centered on some of the central bars creating the variation known as Split Bars.

Creating the **Amish Bars** pattern in a polymer clay cane follows a process very similar to the piecing of a fabric quilt block. The vertical bars are cut from at least two colors. They are carefully measured to create a square central cane. The bars are arranged with alternating colors.

The central square cane is bordered with strips from a third color. This border can be the same thickness as the central strips, or it can be a different thickness to create more interest. Traditionally, square pieces are set in the corners of this border. The corner squares can be made in the color of one of the central strips or can be done in a fourth color.

An additional border completes the quilt cane. This border can also vary in thickness. It can also introduce another color. Corner blocks in this border provide the opportunity for yet another color.

The Amish Bars quilt cane illustrated in the following guidelines is three colors with black accent lines. The finished quilt cane is just under 1½" square, about 4" long. The cane is initially assembled at its finished size. It can be reduced to a very small size without losing visual clarity.

Colors

See Chapter 3 – Color

Clay Preparation

Roll sheets of conditioned clay in three colors (5½" wide, ⅛" thick):
> **Blue** – 8" long
> **Purple** – 4" long
> **Red** – 4" long

Roll six sheets of conditioned **Black** clay, 5½" wide on the <u>thinnest</u> setting possible, at least 4" long. These will provide visual color separation by placing a color rectangle on the black clay and trimming the black to fit.

Blue: Cut one rectangle about 4" wide, 4" long. Back this rectangle on the thin black clay. This will be used for four vertical bars. Cut the second blue rectangle about 5" wide, 4" long. Do <u>not</u> back this second blue rectangle with the black clay. This will be used for the final border.

Purple: Cut one rectangle about 4" wide, 4" long. Back this rectangle on the thin black clay. This will be used for three vertical bars and the corner squares in the first border.

Red: Cut one rectangle about 4" wide, 4" long. Do <u>not</u> back the red rectangle with the black clay. This will be used for the first border strips.

27

Assembling the Amish Bars Central Cane

The vertical bars are cut from the blue and purple colors. They are carefully measured and cut to ⅞" widths. The bars are arranged in alternating colors. Seven bars will create a central cane ⅞" square.

Cut three ⅞" wide, 4" long strips from the purple rectangle and four strips from the blue rectangle with the thin black backing.

Stack these seven strips in alternating colors. Place the black side facing down each time a color strip is added to the stack.

Rotate the cane and place the solid blue side on a sheet of thin black clay. Trim the black clay to fit the side of the cane.

Assembling the First Border

Cut four ⅞" wide, 4" long strips from the red rectangle without the black backing. Cut four ⅛" wide, 4" long strips from the purple with the black backing.

Place a red strip on both sides of the cane as shown.

Place the top of the cane on a sheet of thin black clay and trim to fit. Then place the bottom on the black clay and trim to fit.

Place the tiny purple strips on both ends of a red strip with the black line facing the red end. Do this with both remaining red strips.

Position the top and bottom of the cane on the red and purple assemblage, carefully aligning the corners.

Finishing the Amish Bars Quilt Cane

Cut four blue strips from the blue rectangle without a black backing to finish the last border around the cane. Two of these are 1⅛" wide and 4" long. The other two are 1⅜" wide and 4" long.

Wrap the cane with the thin sheet of black clay by placing each side of the cane on the sheet of black and trimming it to fit.

Place the narrow blue strips on the sides of the cane and the wide blue strips on the top and bottom of the cane. Compress the cane to remove any seams in the blue border.

The finished cane can be wrapped with a thin sheet of black clay. It can be further reduced without losing detail.

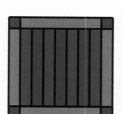

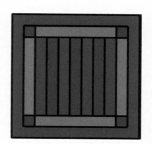

Variations

Monochromatic
Four muted greens without separation lines.

Harvest colors
Differing width borders and corners.

Black, White, Red
A simple arrangement without corner squares.

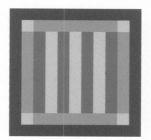

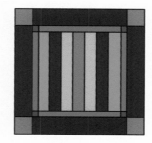

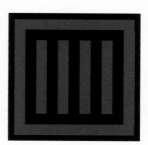

Split Rails
Light coral and dark brown vertical bars.

Varied Width Bars
Three muted colors and a variation in the center.

Simplicity
Black and Brown.

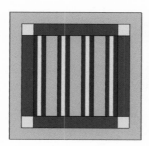

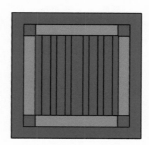

Amish Center Diamond

Quintessentially Amish

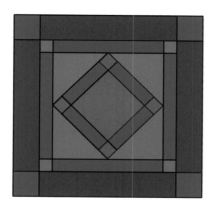

The **Amish Center Diamond** quilt is one of the quintessentially Amish designs. A large square, tipped on its side forms the diamond. It may be bordered or left to float.

Triangles are placed on the sides of the diamond to form another square. This square is bordered and may be anchored with small squares in the corner.

The final border is larger than the inner border(s) and usually are anchored by corner squares. This pattern is also known as Diamond in the Square.

Adapting the **Amish Center Diamond** pattern to polymer clay cane is a straightforward process. The center diamond is carefully cut to form a precise square. It is bordered with strips of a second color with optional corner squares between the strips.

Triangular logs are placed on the sides of the center square. When this assembly is rotated back to a square it shows the Diamond in the Square. This square is again bordered with strips of another color, with optional corner squares between the strips.

A final border completes the quilt cane. This border is usually larger than the other borders. It can also introduce another color. Corner blocks in this border provide the opportunity for yet another color or can repeat one of the interior colors.

The Amish Bars quilt cane illustrated in the guidelines is four colors with black accent lines. The cane is initially assembled just larger than its finished size, about 1¾" square, 4" long. It can be reduced to a very small size without losing visual clarity.

Colors

See Chapter 3 – Color

Clay Preparation

Roll sheets of conditioned clay in four colors (5½" wide, ⅛" thick):

Red – 4" long	**Green** – 4" long
Blue – 4" long	**Purple** – 4" long

Roll six sheets of conditioned **Black** clay, 5½" wide, on the <u>thinnest</u> setting possible, at least 4" long. These will provide visual color separation by placing a color rectangle on the black clay and trimming the black to fit.

Red: Cut one rectangle about 3" wide, 4" long. Cut a second rectangle about 1" wide, 4" long. Back only the 1" wide rectangle on the thin black clay.

Blue: Cut three rectangles. Cut the first rectangle 2½" wide, 4" long. Cut the second rectangle 4½" wide, 4" long. Cut the third rectangle 2½" wide, 4" long. Do <u>not</u> back these with black.

Green: Cut one rectangle about 4½" wide, 4" long. Cut a second rectangle 1" wide, 4" long. Back only the 1" wide rectangle on the thin black clay.

Purple: Cut two rectangles, each about 5½" wide. Stack these sheets together making a single sheet about ¼" thick. Cut a 1" wide, 4" long strip from this stack. Back only the 1" wide rectangle on the thin black clay.

Assembling the Amish Center Diamond

The center diamond is a ½" square log in red clay. The border for the center diamond is four strips of blue with red corner squares. The unusual assembly sequence illustrated in the guidelines will keep a single black separation line between all of the color pieces. For example, if the first red log were wrapped on all sides, the separation between one side of the red corner squares would be missing, or the line on two of the sides of the center diamond would be doubled.

Cut four ½" wide, 4" long strips from the red rectangle without the black backing.

Stack the four red strips into a ½" square log. Smooth the edges of this log until it is precisely square and smooth on all sides..

Place two sides of this log on a sheet of thin black clay. Trim the black clay to fit.

Assembling the Center Diamond Border

Cut four ½" wide, 4" long strips from the blue rectangle. Cut four ⅛" wide, 4" long strips from the red rectangle with the thin black backing.

Place two strips of blue on the sides with the black separation lines.

Place the long sides of this cane on a sheet of thin black clay. Trim the black clay to fit.

Place the tiny red strips on both ends of a blue strip with the black line facing the blue end. Do this with both remaining blue strips.

Position the top and bottom of the cane on the blue and red pieces, carefully aligning the corners.

Place each side of this cane on a sheet of thin black clay. Trim the black clay to fit.

Preparing the Corner Triangles

Cut the green rectangle in half, lengthwise, and stack the strips. Cut it in half again, lengthwise, stack these strips. Cut it in half, crosswise, and stack again. Shape this into a square log, about 2½" long.

Cut this square log on the diagonal into two triangular shaped logs.

Reduce each triangular log until the diagonal is ¾". Match the sides of the center diamond for the exact size. Cut each log in half for the four triangles.

Assembling the Central Square

Cut four 1" wide, 4" long strips from the blue rectangle. Cut four ⅛" wide, 4" long strips from the green rectangle with the black backing.

Place the triangular logs on all sides of the center cane. Reduce this to a 1" square cane. Trim the ends to a 4" long cane.

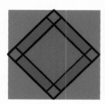

Place two sides of this cane on a sheet of thin black clay. Trim the black clay to fit.

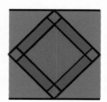

Place two strips of blue on the sides with the black.

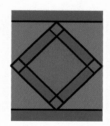

Place the long sides of this cane on a sheet of thin black clay. Trim the black clay to fit.

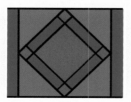

Place the tiny green strips on both ends of a blue strip with the black line facing the blue end. Do this with both remaining blue strips.

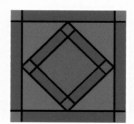

Position the top and bottom of the cane on the blue and green assemblages, carefully aligning the corners.

Finishing the Amish Center Diamond Quilt Cane

The outer border of an Amish Center Diamond quilt is usually much wider than the inner borders as this portion will hang down the sides of a bed keeping the main pattern centered on the bed. For a polymer clay cane, the outer border can be the same size as the inner border or somewhat larger and still present the same dramatic pattern. These guidelines create a double width outer border.

Cut four 1¼" wide, 4" long strips from the double thickness purple rectangle. Cut four ¼" wide, 4" long strips from the double thickness blue rectangle with the black backing.

Place two sides of this cane on a sheet of thin black clay. Trim the black clay to fit.	Place two of the double thickness strips of purple on the sides with the black.	Place the long sides of this cane on a sheet of thin black clay. Trim the black clay to fit.

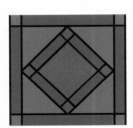

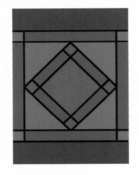

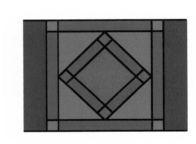

Place the small blue strips on both ends of a purple strip with the black line facing the purple end. Do this with both remaining purple strips.	Position the top and bottom of the cane on the purple and blue assemblages, carefully aligning the corners. The cane will be about 1¾" square.	If desired, wrap the finished cane with a thin sheet of black clay. Reduce the cane to 1½" square. It can be reduced to a cane as small as ¾" square without losing detail.

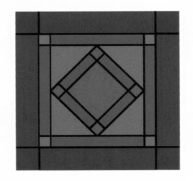

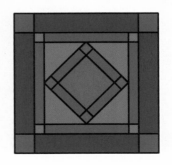

Variations

This simple pattern can have a wealth of variety. These examples have different border widths and color combinations. They also illustrate the difference created by a simple black line between colors.

Without Black Lines
The same colors without black separation lines.

Brighter Colors
Three colors with varying width borders and corners.

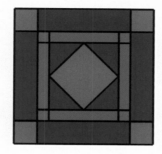

Monochromatic
A simple arrangement with varied width borders.

Harvest colors
Muted colors, varied width borders, no separation lines.

Two Colors
Fixed width borders and black corners.

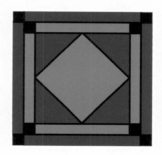

Two Colors
The simplest arrangement without corner squares.

Brilliant Colors
Neon colors with black corners and separation lines.

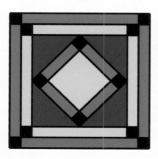

Muted Colors
Fixed width borders and corners and separation lines.

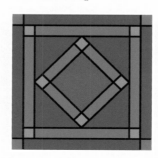

Black, White and Red
Banded center diamond with interesting black corners.

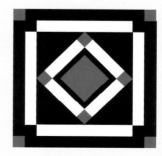

Nine~Patch

Intriguing Variations

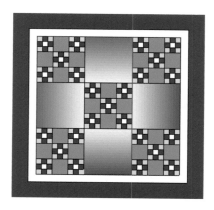

The **Nine-Patch** is one of the simplest of all quilt blocks consisting of nine squares arranged three-by-three. It is also one of the most versatile blocks; the variations are almost limitless. While simple, the possibilities are intriguing.

Seldom are all the patches in a quilt done in the same color scheme. With the small pieces and numerous color possibilities, it is an excellent pattern for a scrap quilt.

This pattern was likely a first choice for many girls beginning their piecing skills.

Adapting the **Nine-Patch** pattern to polymer clay cane is a very rewarding process making full use of polymer clay's *millefiore* capabilities. The simple Nine-Patch block is assembled in two colors in a three-by-three checkerboard pattern. This block cane can be used by itself with a simple border. The guidelines include a finished block cane, about 1" square, 4" long.

The Nine-Patch block cane is reduced and cut into five equal segments. It is then assembled with four blocks of solid color forming a Double Nine-Patch cane. This cane can also be used by itself with a border. The guidelines include a finished Double Nine-Patch cane, about 1½" square, 4" long.

The Double Nine-Patch block cane is reduced and cut into five segments. It is combined with a blended log for a finished Nine-Patch quilt cane. A final border completes the quilt cane.

The Nine-Patch quilt cane illustrated in the following guidelines is done in four colors with black accent lines. The quilt cane is initially assembled just larger than its finished size, about 1½" square, 4" long. Reducing the quilt cane to a much smaller size will lose visual clarity.

Colors

See Chapter 3 – Color

Clay Preparation

Roll sheets of conditioned clay in three colors (5½" wide, ⅛" thick):

Brown – 13" long	**White** – 9" long
Ecru – 9" long	**Teal** – 9" long

These sheets will be rolled to different thicknesses and cut into rectangles during the cane assembly processes.

Roll eight sheets of conditioned **Black** clay, 5½" wide on the <u>thinnest</u> setting possible, at least 4" long. These will provide visual color separation by placing a color rectangle on the black clay and trimming the black to fit.

Cut 4" from the white and teal for a **Four-Section Skinner Blend.** Cut each of these into four equal width four rectangles, 1⅜" wide, 4" long. Cut them into triangles by cutting corner to corner. Position the triangles as shown. Complete the blending process as detailed in *Chapter 3 – Color.*

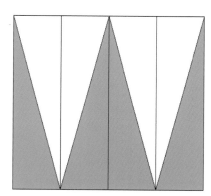

Assembling the Nine-Patch Block Cane

The block cane is a simple three-by-three cane in a checkerboard pattern. The starting squares are ½" square, 4" long. They are assembled into a cane 1½" square. This cane is first reduced to a ¾" square cane about 16" long. A 4" segment is cut from one end. This segment is then wrapped with a border for a finished cane. The rest of the block cane is further reduced to a cane ½" square, over 25" long. This will be used in the Double Nine-Patch cane.

Cut four strips 2" wide, 4" long from the brown clay.

Stack the four brown strips into a ½" thick stack. Place the stack on the thin black clay. Trim the black clay to fit.

Cut this stack into four ½" wide, 4" long strips. Smooth the edges if necessary without changing the size.

Cut four 2" wide, 4" long strips from the ecru clay.

Stack the four ecru strips into a ½" thick stack. Place this stack on the thin black clay. Trim the black clay to fit.

Cut this stack into four ½" wide, 4" long strips. Smooth the edges if necessary without changing the size.

Cut four ½" wide, 4" long strips from the white clay.

Stack the four white strips into a ½" thick stack. Place this stack on the thin black clay. Trim the black clay to fit.

Arrange the strips in three rows of three. Be sure the black lines are in the positions shown.

Place the long sides of each row on a sheet of thin black clay. Trim the black clay to fit.

Stack the three rows together, carefully matching the corners.

Finishing the Nine-Patch Block Cane

Place the two sides that are not black on a sheet of thin black clay. Trim the black clay to fit. Reduce the cane to ¾" square, about 16" long. Trim one cane end and cut off a 4" segment for use in the block cane.

Roll a sheet of white clay on a medium setting about 4" long. Place each side of this block cane on the white clay. Trim the white clay to fit. Compress the cane and smooth the seams.

Roll a sheet of brown clay on a thicker setting, 4" long. Place each side of the cane on the brown clay and trim to fit. Again, compress the cane and smooth the seams.

Assembling the Double Nine-Patch Cane

Reduce the remaining Nine-Patch block cane to ½" square, over 25" long. Trim the waste ends from this cane. Cut the cane into five equal segments, each about 5" long.

Cut four strips 2" wide, 4" long from the teal rectangles.

Stack the four teal strips into a ½" thick stack. Do not place this stack on the black clay.

Cut this stack into four ½" wide, 4" long strips. Smooth the edges if necessary without changing the size.

Arrange the strips in three rows of three strips.

Stack the three rows together, carefully matching the corners.

Place each side of the cane on a sheet of thin black clay and trim the black clay to fit.

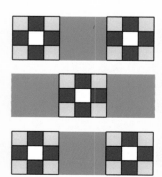

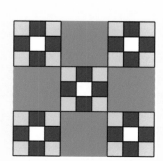

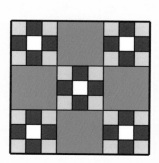

Finishing the Double Nine-Patch Cane

Reduce the cane to a 1" square, about 11" long. Trim the ends slightly. Cut 4" from one end for the finished Double Nine-Patch block cane.

Roll a sheet of white clay on a medium setting, about 4" long. Place each side of this block cane on the white clay. Trim the clay to fit. Compress the cane and smooth the seams.

Roll a sheet of brown clay on a thicker setting, 4" long. Place each side of the cane on the brown clay and trim to fit. Again, compress the cane and smooth the seams.

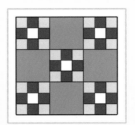

Assembling the Full Nine-Patch Cane

Reduce the rest of the Double Nine-Patch block cane to ½" square, over 20" long. Trim the waste ends from this cane. Cut the cane into five equal segments, each about 4" long.

Prepare a 8" long sheet of a four section Skinner Blend with the teal and white clay. Cut this sheet crosswise into four 2" sections. Stack these sheets into a ½" thick rectangle as shown. See *Chapter 3 – Color* for Skinner Blend details.

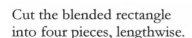

Cut the blended rectangle into four pieces, lengthwise.

Compress this into a ½" square log.

Arrange the strips in three rows of three strips.

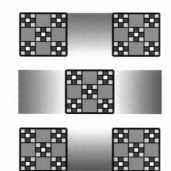

Stack the three rows together carefully matching the corners.

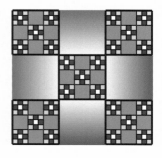

Finishing the Full Nine-Patch Quilt Cane

Place each side of the cane on a sheet of thin black clay, and trim the black clay to fit.

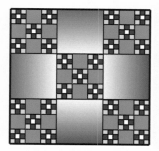

Roll a sheet of white clay on a medium setting, about 4" long. Place each side of this block cane on the white clay. Trim the clay to fit.

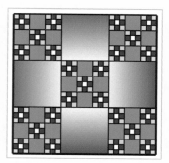

Roll a sheet of brown clay on a thicker setting. Place each side of the cane on the brown clay and trim to fit. Reduce the cane as desired, smoothing the seams.

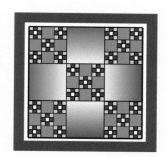

Variations

White Crosses

Small changes with interesting results. The Nine-Patch block cane has dark corners and light centers. There are no black separation lines.

Notice the appearance of white crosses. Also, the Nine-Patch blocks seem to be larger.

Red, White and Blue

Nine-Patch block, Double Nine-Patch block, full quilt Pattern.

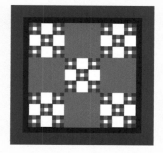

Double Nine-Patch

Floral cane highlights.

Black, White and Red

Striking use of black, white and red in Nine-Patch and Double Nine-Patch blocks with a bold geometric or a subtle pattern.

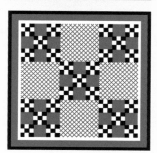

Nine-Patch Variation

Corners of Interest

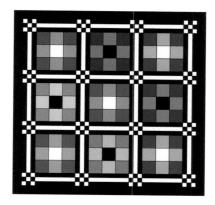

This variation of the **Nine-Patch** quilt pattern is a multi-color delight. In keeping with tradition, the larger Nine-Patch blocks are done in many different colors.

The striped banding between the Nine-Patches has a tiny black and white Nine-Patch block set in the corners of the rows of banding. The center square of the color Nine-Patch blocks is also done in black and white reflecting the tiny banding Nine-Patches.

This is truly a quilt to use up those scraps.

There are three versions of this cane presented in the guidelines. All versions use nine colors in two values for the larger Nine-Patches. The darker values are used for the corner patches. These colors are each mixed with white for the lighter patches. The center patch color varies in the examples. These steps create nine monochromatic Nine-Patch canes 5" long, with half reserved for individual Nine-Patch canes or future projects.

The feature cane, as shown above, requires careful precision in cane assembly and reduction. It is, however, a delightful accomplishment. The finished cane is 1½" square and almost 8" long. It can be reduced to less than 1" square without losing visual clarity.

The second version uses simple rows of solid black banding with dark grey corner squares in the banding. The center squares of the color Nine-Patches are a lighter grey.

The simplest version simply separates all color Nine-Patches with black banding.

Color selection and arrangement is a challenging part of making Nine-Patch Quilt canes.

Colors

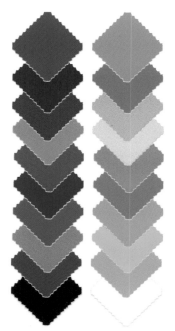

See Chapter 3 – Color

Clay Preparation (Feature Cane)

Roll sheets of conditioned clay in nine colors, black, and white (5½" wide, on the thickest setting, ⅛" thick):

Darker Colors – 5" long
Black – 16" long
White – 24" long

Mix one third of each color with an equal amount of white for the lighter colors. Roll all of the colors into sheets, 5½" wide, 2" long, ⅛" thick.

Roll six sheets of conditioned **Black** clay, 5½" wide on the <u>thinnest</u> setting possible, at least 5" long. These will provide visual color separation by placing a color rectangle on the black clay and trimming the black to fit.

Colors: Cut two rectangles from each color sheet for the Nine-Patch canes, each 1" wide, 5" long .

Black: Cut two rectangles 3" wide, 5" long.

White: Cut two rectangles 3" wide, 5" long.

The remaining Black and White clay will be rolled on thinner settings for the bands between the Nine-Patches when needed as described in the guidelines.

Assembling the Nine-Patch Block Cane

Each Nine-Patch block cane is a simple three-by-three cane in a checkerboard pattern. The starting squares are ¼" square, 5 long. They are assembled into canes ¾" square, 5" long. Segments measuring 2½" long are cut from one end of each cane and wrapped with a border for finished Nine-Patch block canes.

Cutting Black and White Centers for the Color Nine-Patch Canes

Cut two strips black, 1" wide, 5" long and two strips white, 1¼" wide, 5" long.

Stack each pair of two strips into a ¼" thick stack. Place the stack on the thin black clay. Trim to fit.

Cut each stack into five ¼" wide, 5" long strips. Smooth the edges if necessary without changing the size.

Cutting Color Squares for Each Color Nine-Patch Cane

Use two strips 1" wide, 5" long from both colors of clay for each nine-patch cane.

Stack each pair of two strips into a ¼" thick stack. Place the stack on the thin black clay. Trim to fit.

Cut each stack into four ¼" wide, 5" long strips. Smooth the edges if necessary without changing the size.

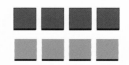

Assembling Color Nine-Patch Canes

Arrange the strips in three rows of three. Be sure the black lines are in the positions shown.

Place the long sides of each row on a sheet of thin black clay. Trim the black clay to fit.

Stack the rows together carefully matching the corners. Place the two sides that are not black on the thin black clay. Trim to fit.

The Other Color Nine-Patch Canes

Finishing the Color Nine-Patch Block Canes

Cut the Nine-Patch canes into two equal segments, saving one set for the feature cane and using the rest for finished Nine-Patch canes or for future projects.

Roll a sheet of white or black clay on a medium setting about 2½" long. Place each side of the block cane on this clay. Trim to fit. Compress the cane and smooth the seams.

Roll a sheet of the darker color clay on a thicker setting, about 2½" long. Place each side of the cane on the darker color clay and trim to fit. Compress the cane and smooth the seams.

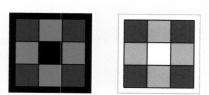

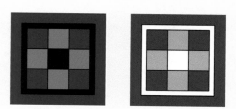

Assembling the Black and White Nine-Patch Block Canes

Assemble a black and white Nine-Patch cane following the same process as the color Nine-Patch canes, except the thin black clay for color separation is not necessary in this step. When reduced, this is just enough for the tiny corner Nine-Patches in the border. Be prepared to make an additional cane if this doesn't reduce as well as anticipated!

Cut two strips black, 1" wide, 5" long and two strips white, 1¼" wide, 5" long.

Stack the strips and cut each stack into ¼" wide, 5" long strips. Smooth the edges if necessary without changing the size.

Stack the strips into rows and stack the rows together, carefully matching the corners.

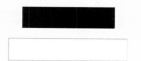

Preparing the Banding Pieces for the Feature Cane

Find a thickness on the pasta machine where three sheets of clay, stacked are just under ¼" thick. Roll one rectangle of white and two rectangles of black clay on this setting, each sheet 9" long, 5" wide. Cut this stack into two strips, each 9" long, 2½" wide.

Cut 24 strips from this stack exactly the same width as the color Nine-Patch canes. They should all be ¾" wide, 2½" long.

Reduce the black and white nine-patch cane to a tiny cane, just under ¼" square. This cane is the same thickness as the border stack. As this will reduce to a total length of 45", cut it in half when it gets too long to reduce easily and work with sections. This will be cut into 16 pieces, 2½" long.

Assembling the Sections of Feature Cane

Each color Nine-Patch is assembled with at least two strips of the black and white banding and one tiny black and white corner Nine-Patch cane.

Assemble one strip of banding and one Nine-Patch cane.

Assemble the tiny Nine-Patch corner cane with a strip of banding.

Position the two assemblage together, carefully aligning the corners.

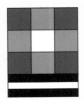

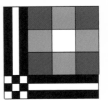

Assemble each color Nine-Patch section following the same process, as illustrated below. The side pieces have an additional banding and corner strip; the lower corner section also has an assembly of two tiny Nine-Patch corner canes and a strip of banding.

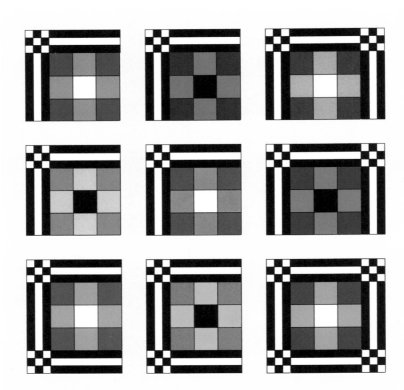

These sections can be assembled into a finished cane 3¼" square by about 2½" long and reduced to about 1½" by 10" long. Anticipate some waste with a cane this size.

An alternative method is to carefully reduce each section and then assemble them into a finished cane. With this method it is important to maintain the rectangular aspect on the bottom row and right side.

Finishing the Feature Quilt Cane

Assemble three rows of three Nine-Patch sections as shown. Position the rows together, carefully aligning the corners. Reduce the cane to about 1½" square, about 8" long.

Roll a sheet of black clay on a medium setting large enough to wrap the entire cane. Place each side of the cane on this sheet and trim to fit. Reduce the cane as desired, smoothing the seams. This cane can be reduced to less than 1" square without losing visual clarity.

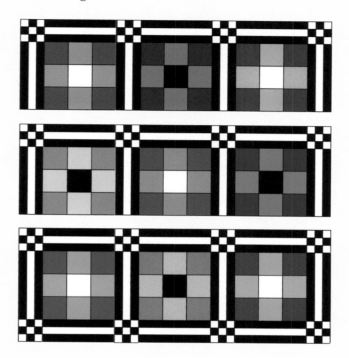

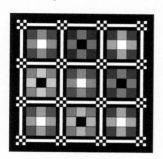

Minimal Color Changes with Visible Results

Center Nine-Patch Colors
This replaces the black and white Nine-Patch center squares with the color used in the corners.

Brown and Ecru
The same colors in the Nine-Patch with brown and ecru banding.

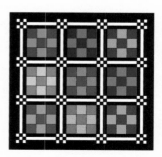

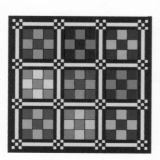

Assembling the Second Variation

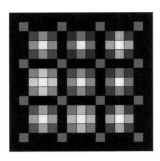

This variation uses a light grey center in all of the color Nine-Patch canes. The banding is done with black banding and darker grey corner squares. The color Nine-Patch canes are reduced to ⅜" square canes before adding the banding. This variation starts and ends with a much smaller cane.

The banding strips are cut from a sheet of black clay rolled on the thickest setting. The corner squares are cut from a sheet of dark grey clay rolled on the thickest setting.

Assemble nine color Nine-Patch canes as illustrated on the previous pages. Reduce these canes to ⅜" square. Cut 24 ⅜" wide strips the length of the color Nine-Patch canes. Cut a rectangle of dark grey clay about 3" wide, also the length of the canes.

Assemble one strip of banding and one Nine-Patch cane.

Place a strip of banding next to the rectangle of dark grey clay. Firmly press into position.

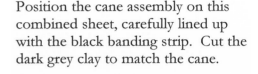

Position the cane assembly on this combined sheet, carefully lined up with the black banding strip. Cut the dark grey clay to match the cane.

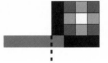

Assemble each Nine-Patch section following the same process shown for the feature quilt, as illustrated below. The side pieces have an additional banding and corner strip; the lower corner section also has an additional banding strip with two corners.

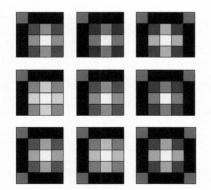

Assemble these sections into three rows of three, stack the rows, carefully aligning the corners.

Add a black border to finish the cane shown in the upper left corner of this page.

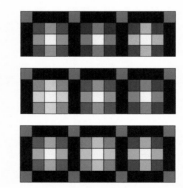

Color Variations

More Subtle Centers
Color Nine-Patch centers

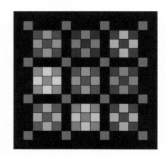

High Contrast White
Black Nine-Patch centers white banding corners

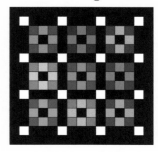

Assembling the Third Variation

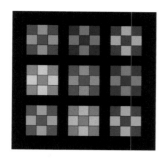

This variation is the simplest to construct and perhaps the most dramatic in its finished appearance. The color Nine-Patch canes are surrounded with black and assembled into a cane. Another black border finishes the Nine-Patch quilt cane.

Assemble nine color Nine-Patch canes as illustrated on the previous pages. Reduce these canes to ½" square. Roll two sheets of black clay on a medium setting, 5½" wide, as long as the canes.

Place each side of the Nine-Patch canes on the sheet of black clay. Trim the black clay to fit the cane.

Assemble these sections into three rows of three. Assemble the rows into a cane. Add a black border to complete the cane shown in the upper left corner of this page.

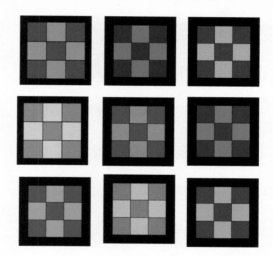

Color Variations

Black Center Squares

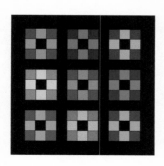

White Banding

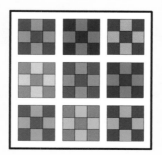

White Banding
White center squares.

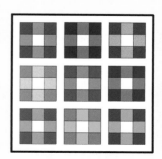

Log Cabin

Playing with Light and Dark

Log Cabin quilts are patterned after the construction of pioneer houses on the frontier. Rough logs were laid on top of each other around the center of the building, in the same way fabric strips are placed in rows around a center square which is traditionally red to signify the hearth.

Log Cabin blocks are usually constructed with a strong light and dark contrast with the block divided diagonally. The rotation of the blocks creates a wealth of intriguing variations.

Creating the Log Cabin pattern in a polymer clay cane follows a process very similar to the piecing of a fabric quilt block. The center square log is placed on a sheet of the innermost color and the color is cut to size. This assembly is rotated, placed on the same color sheet, and again cut to match. This is repeated through a series of colors to form an initial cane representing a single Log Cabin block. These block canes are reduced and arranged to create secondary patterns.

Common Log Cabin patterns include: Barn Raising, in which the blocks are arranged as concentric bands of diamond shaped color; Light and Dark, with four dark areas side-by-side so the light areas are also juxtaposed; Straight Furrow, with its diagonal lines evoking plowed fields; and Streak of Lightning with strong zig-zag lines. It is important to maintain a high light and dark contrast or the secondary designs are lost.

Two initial Log Cabin block canes are illustrated in the guidelines, using four values of an olive-green and four values of blue, both lightened with ivory. These block canes can create two Log Cabin quilt canes about 1½" square, 3" long with several smaller canes in a variety of patterns.

Colors

See *Chapter 3 – Color*

Clay Preparation

Roll sheets of conditioned clay in eight colors (5½" wide, ⅛" thick):
    Olives and Blues – 4" long for cane
    Border Colors – Additional 4" long to wrap canes
    Red – 1" long

Roll eight sheets of conditioned **Black** clay, 5½" wide on the <u>thinnest</u> setting possible, at least 6" long. These will provide visual color separation by placing a color rectangle on the black clay and trimming the black to fit.

Olives and Blues: Cut a rectangle about 3" wide, 6" long from each color. Back this rectangle on the thin black clay.

Red: Do <u>not</u> back the red rectangle with black. Cut two strips each ⅛" wide for the center square of each cane.

The pieces shown on the facing page include the olive-blue canes presented in these guidelines, rust-brown canes and a black-white-grey cane. The black and white cane started with a more visible ¼" center square of red. For this center square size, the black, white and grey rectangles were 3½" wide, 6" long.

Assembling the Log Cabin Block Canes

Lay out the eight sheets of clay in the order the cane will be assembled. Place the rectangles with the black side up. The first cane has the olive values in the center, blues on the outside; the second is reversed. The color sequence for the first cane is: Pale Olive, Olive, Medium Olive, Dark Olive, Pale Blue, Blue, Medium Blue, Dark Blue. The second cane is exactly reversed. Two pieces will be cut from each color sheet while assembling the block cane.

Place the thin Red strip on the black side of the first color, pale olive. Cut the color sheet to exactly match the red strip. Lightly press pieces together.

Rotate the piece a quarter turn; place it on the same color, pale olive. Cut the color to match. Lightly press together.

Repeat with the next color, olive

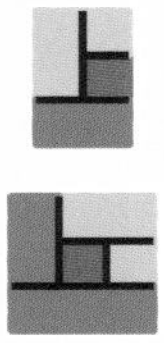

Medium Olive

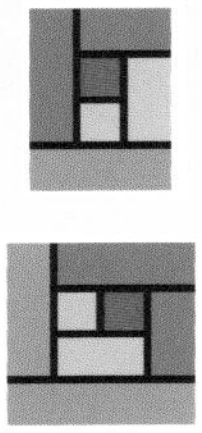

Dark Olive

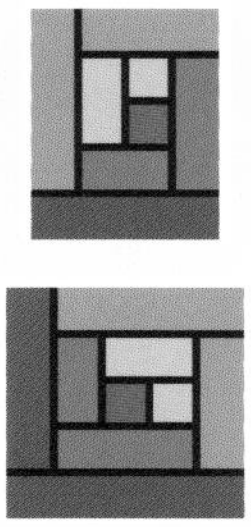

Light Blue

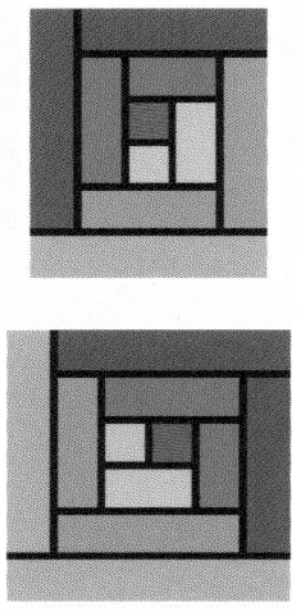

Blue

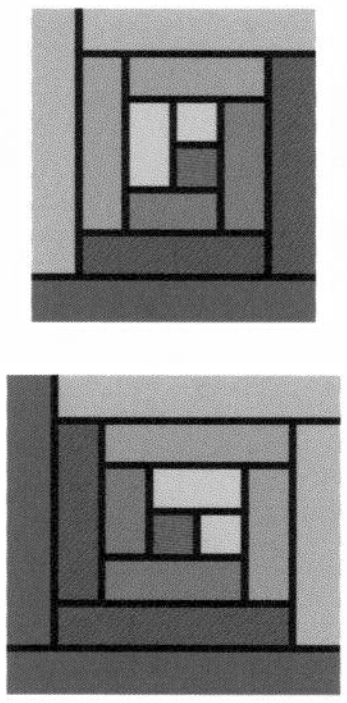

Medium Blue

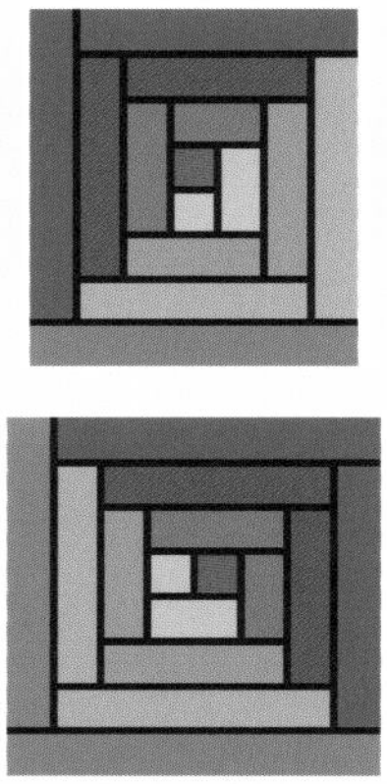

Dark Blue

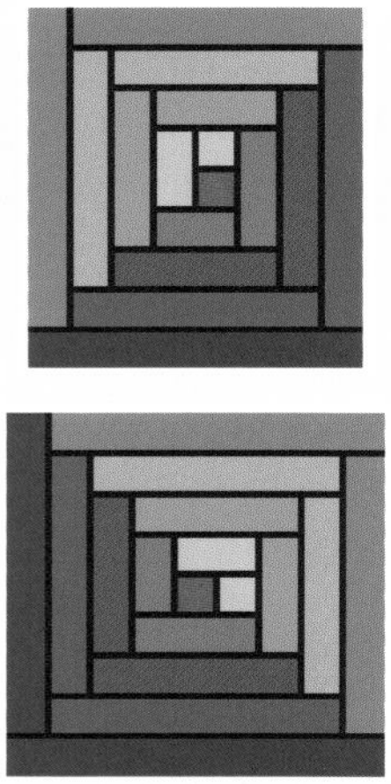

Place each side of the cane on a very thin sheet of black. Cut the black clay to fit the cane side.

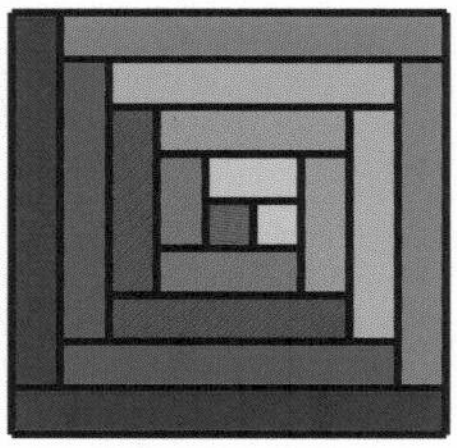

Reduce this cane until it is about ½" square. It will be about 24" long when reduced.

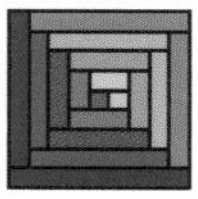

Make a second Log Cabin block cane with the remaining color sheets, reversing the color sequence.

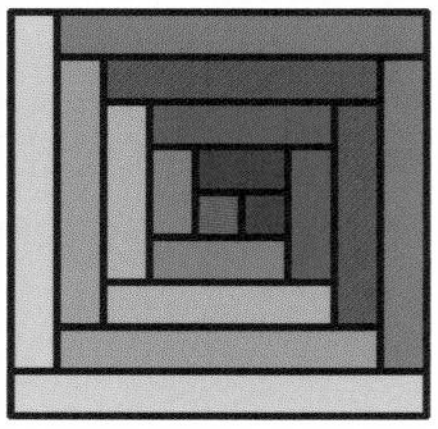

Reduce this cane until it is about ½" square. It will be about 24" long when reduced.

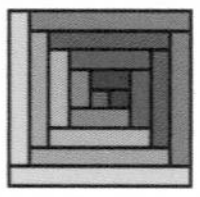

The Log Cabin Quilt Canes

The most difficult part of assembling a Log Cabin Quilt cane is deciding which pattern to make.

For the **Barn Raising** pattern, the second cane is assembled from nine block cane segments arranged in a strong diagonal pattern. Four segments of this cane create the full quilt pattern.

In **Furrows**, the second cane has four block cane segments creating a diagonal pattern. Assembling segments of the second cane continues the strong diagonal in the full quilt pattern.

Light and Dark has a center diamond made with four block cane segments in the second cane, with segments of the second cane creating a diagonal checkerboard effect.

For **Streak of Lightning**, the second cane is a carat or "V" shape assembled with four block cane segments. Segments of the second cane are assembled into a zig-zag pattern.

Barn Raising	**Furrows**	**Light & Dark**	**Streak of Lightning**

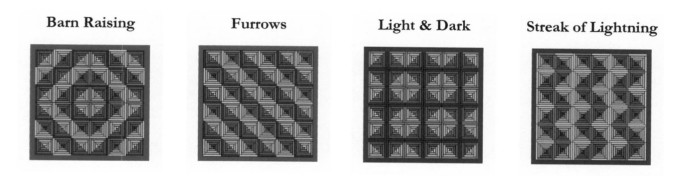

Assembling the Second Barn Raising Pattern Cane

Cut five segments from the first block cane with Blue on the outside, and four segments from the other block cane with Olive on the outside, about 3" long. Save the remaining block canes for another pattern.

Assemble these segments into three rows of three segments each. Alternate the canes as shown below. Carefully align the corners in these rows.

Assemble these rows into one cane, again carefully aligning the corners when arranging the rows.

Reduce this cane to about ¾" square, about 12" long. Trim most of the waste from both ends of the cane.

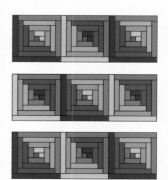

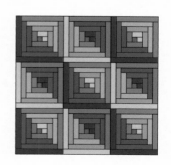

Finishing the Barn Raising Quilt Cane

Cut the second Barn Raising cane into four equal segments about 3" long.

Assemble these into two rows. Then put the two rows together, aligning the corners in the center. Reduce this cane until there is not a gap in the center.

Wrap the cane with a sheet of border color, rolled on a medium setting. Reduce the finished cane to 1½" square.

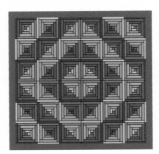

This is the same pattern, using the same second canes with the dark corners in the center and a different border.

Variations in Color and Arrangement

Color selection and the center diamond arrangement are important in the Barn Raising pattern.

Reds and Browns
Closer color values result in stronger diamonds.

Four color ways
Combining several block cane colors makes intricate patterns.

Black, White and Greys
A larger red center creates dramatic variations.

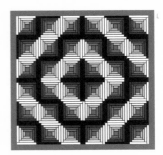

Assembling the Second Furrows Quilt Cane

Cut two segments from each of the original block canes, each about 5" long.

Assemble these segments into two rows of two segments each, alternating the canes as shown.

Assemble these two rows into one cane, again carefully aligning the corners when arranging the rows.

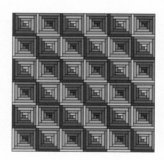

Reduce this cane to about ½" square. It will be about 20" long. Trim most of the waste from both ends of the cane.

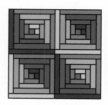

Finishing the Furrows Quilt Cane

Cut the second Furrows cane into nine segments, about 2" long. Assemble them into three rows of three segments as shown.

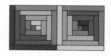

Assemble these rows into one cane, again carefully aligning the corners when arranging the rows.

Wrap the cane with a sheet of border color, rolled on a medium setting. Reduce the finished cane to 1½" square.

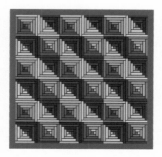
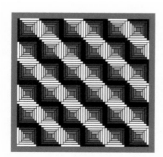

Color Variations

Assembling the Second Light and Dark Quilt Cane

Cut two segments from one of the original block canes, each about 4" long.

Assemble these segments into two rows of two segments each, arranging the canes as shown.

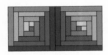

Assemble these two rows into one cane, again carefully aligning the corners when arranging the rows.

Reduce this cane to about ½" square. It will be about 16" long. Trim most of the waste from both ends of the cane.

Finishing the Light and Dark Quilt Cane

Cut this cane into four segments, about 4" long. Assemble into two rows of two segments.

Assemble these rows into one cane, again carefully aligning the corners.

Wrap the cane with a sheet of border color, rolled on a medium setting. Reduce the finished cane to 1" square.

Variations in Color and Configuration

Reds and Browns
Three rows of three with high contrast colors.

Four Color Blocks
More intricate patterns.

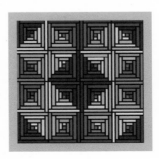

Black, White, Greys
A large red center creates dramatic shading.

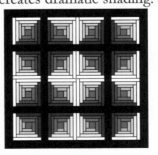

Assembling the Second Strike of Lightning Quilt Cane

Cut four segments from one of the original block canes, each about 4" long.

Assemble these segments into two rows of two segments, alternating the canes as shown.

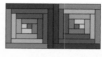

Assemble these two rows into one cane, again carefully aligning the corners when arranging the rows.

Reduce this cane to about ½" square, it will be about 16" long. Trim most of the waste from both ends of the cane.

Finishing the Strike of Lightning Quilt Cane

Cut this cane into four segments, each about 4" long. Assemble into two rows of two segments.

Assemble these rows into one cane, again carefully aligning the corners when arranging the rows.

Wrap the cane with a sheet of border color, rolled on a medium setting. Reduce the finished cane to 1" square.

Variations in Color and Configuration

Reds and Browns
Three rows of three with high contrast in colors.

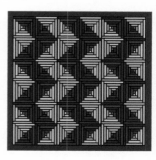

Four Color Blocks
More intricate patterns.

Black, White, Greys
A large red center creates dramatic shading.

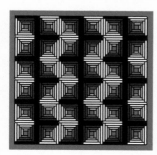

Lone Star

A Quilt with Many Names

This old multi-pieced star is known by many names. The **Mathematical Star** was an early name used in England and in the Eastern US, especially near Baltimore. **Star of Bethlehem** and **Star of the East**, are known all around the country. **Morning Star** comes from the Native Americans, and **Lone Star** comes from Texan quilters.

The pattern has a large central star pieced from diamond shapes. Colors are chosen to form concentric circles radiating around the center. Tiny stars, flowers and other patterns are often placed in the large blank areas surrounding the star.

Creating a Lone Star quilt cane in polymer clay can be quite a challenge given the diamond shape. The cane is composed of a series of diamond shaped pieces, assembled into one large cane. This diamond shaped cane is reduced, cut in half, and assembled with a square cane in the corner and two triangles completing a square. The square cane is easily reduced, cut into four segments and assembled into the center star. Final border pieces complete the quilt cane.

Creating the initial diamond shaped cane can be done three different ways. The easiest is using an extruder and a diamond shaped die, the one with a 45° angle at the point.

Without an extruder, a diamond shape can be formed from two triangular logs, placed back to back. These diamond shaped logs can be reduced, assembled into the larger diamond pattern and then carefully formed into the exact 45° diamond shape.

The strangest method for creating the pattern starts as a square cane, composed of square logs. The square can be transformed into a diamond shape in the reduction process. Using this as a starting cane is the only easy way to include a thin black line of clay to visually separate the colors.

Colors

See Chapter 3—Color

Clay Preparation

Roll sheets of conditioned clay in eight colors (5½" wide, ⅛" thick):

Teal – 2¾" long	**Gold** – 3½" long
Tan – 3½" long	**Red** – 2" long
Lt Teal – 4" long	**Coral** – 2" long
Blue – 3½" long	**Brown** – 2¾" long

When using a polymer clay extruder, the clay must be conditioned until it is quite soft. Roll the clay into logs which fit into the extruder.

Roll a sheet of conditioned clay in the dark brown color for the final cane wrap, 8" long, 5½" wide, on a medium setting.

Roll additional sheets of gold and brown for the corner blends, each 5" long, 5½" wide, ⅛" thick. Prepare a standard two-color Skinner Blend using these sheets.

Details for blending are in *Chapter 3 — Color.*

Assembling the Diamond Cane

This pattern is assembled from eight colors of diamonds in 36 individual diamond strips. The colors are arranged in six rows of six, carefully following a color layout. The rows are assembled, aligning corners and again, closely following the color layout. This diamond shaped cane is reduced to about 8" long and cut into two segments. These segments are assembled with a square corner and two triangles to complete a square cane about 4" long. This is reduced to about 12" long, cut into four segments and reassembled into the center star.

Extrude 36 equal length diamond shapes in these colors:

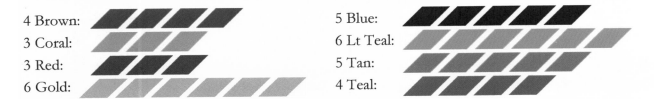

4 Brown:		5 Blue:	
3 Coral:		6 Lt Teal:	
3 Red:		5 Tan:	
6 Gold:		4 Teal:	

Assemble these diamond shapes into six rows of six diamonds each:

Assemble these rows into the larger diamond shape carefully aligning the corners.

Reduce this cane to a workable size, no more than 2" from tip to tip, about 6" long. Cut the cane into two segments. Select either end of the diamond for the center and position the segments together.

60

Preparing the Corner Blend

Prepare a Skinner Blend sheet of Gold and Brown, 10" long, 5½" wide. Roll this into a bulls-eye cane 2" long. (See *Chapter 3 – Color* for details on this process.) Shape this into a square cane.

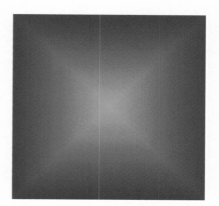

Roll a rectangle of Brown large enough to wrap this bulls-eye cane. Place each side of the cane on the Brown sheet and cut to fit. Compress the cane. Cut down through the cane as shown to create two square logs and four triangular logs.

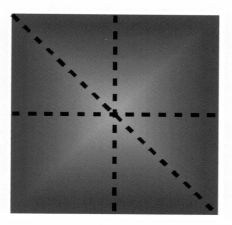

Attach the two square logs end-to-end into a single piece. Attach both pairs of triangular logs end-to-end into single pieces.

Place the blended corner log between the two points of the star. Place the blended triangular logs on both sides of the points of the star. Check that the dark edges of the blended logs are on the outside. This forms a square cane.

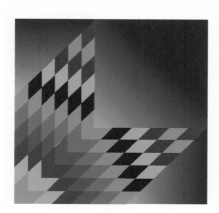

Reduce the cane to about 1" square. Cut into four equal segments. Assemble the segments to form the center star.

Finishing the Lone Star Quilt Cane

The border around the Lone Star Quilt may be as simple as shown in these guidelines, may include more corner blocks or may be made from more intricate patterns.

Place each side of the cane on a sheet of brown clay rolled on a medium setting, cut to fit. Reduce the finished cane to about 1½" square.

Creating the Diamond Logs Without an Extruder

Using the full amount of clay indicated in Clay Preparation, form a triangular shaped log. Cut this log in half and place the backs together to form a diamond shape.

Reduce these diamond shaped logs into logs at least 6" long for each color section. The diamond can be elongated either during this reduction, or during the reduction of the full diamond cane. Continue the process shown on the previous pages.

Creating the Diamond Logs from a Square Log

Assemble a square cane using ¼" square logs in the same color sequence shown for the diamond cane.

Reduce the cane while reshaping it into a diamond. Press near, but not on the corners to work it into the desired shape.

Continue reducing until the diamond is the correct shape. Two sections of the cane will form a right angle when placed together. Continue the process as shown on the previous pages.

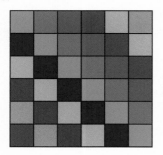

Variations

This simple pattern can have a wealth of variety. These examples have different border widths and color combinations. They also illustrate the difference created by a simple black line between colors.

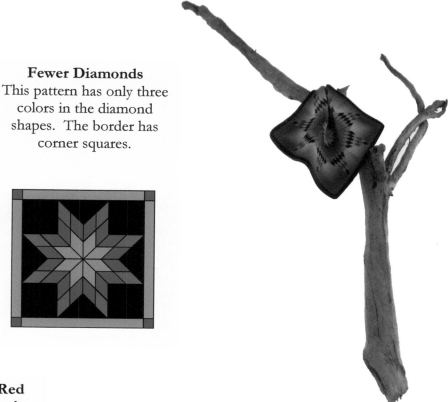

Fewer Diamonds
This pattern has only three colors in the diamond shapes. The border has corner squares.

Black, White and Red
Corner blocks in simple radiating squares sets off the center star.

Corner Stars
A rainbow of colors with simpler stars set in the corner blocks..

Sunshine & Shadow

Light and Shade in the Field

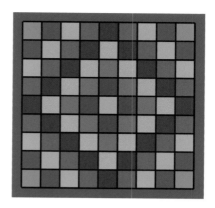

Sunshine & Shadow is perhaps the best known quilt pattern using only squares. Rows of colored squares radiate out from the central square in bands of contrasting hues. The pattern gets its name from the light and dark effect created by the harmonizing and juxtaposition of a large number of bold solid colors. The result may be a subtle blending or a dramatic opposition of light and dark.

This pattern may be done in printed fabrics by non-Amish quilters and known as **Trip Around the World**.

Creating the **Sunshine & Shadow** pattern in a polymer clay cane is simple in concept and design. However, as with its fabric counterpart, it requires many little pieces, carefully organized for assembly. The pattern shown here is 9 rows of 9 pieces, 81 total. On the facing page, the blue, red and purple pattern is 31 by 31 (961 pieces). For a more realistic project, the green, yellow and purple is 11 by 11 (121 pieces).

It is possible to assemble a quadrant of the Sunshine & Shadow cane, reduce it and reassemble the quadrants into the full quilt pattern. The trick is retaining the single rows in the center of the design. This is discussed in the guidelines as an option. Photographs of this process can be seen in *Chapter 4 – Elements of Caning.*

The Sunshine & Shadow quilt cane illustrated in the guidelines uses three values of three colors with black accent lines. The assembled quilt cane is just over 1" square, about 4" long. The cane is initially assembled just larger than its finished size. It can be reduced to a very small size without losing visual clarity. Again, notice the reduction of the pieces on the facing page.

Colors

Clay Preparation

Roll sheets of conditioned clay in nine colors (5½" wide, ⅛" thick):
  Blue – 4" long
  Teal – 4" long
  Green – 4" long
  White (or Off-white) – 4" long
  Black – 8" long

Cut a rectangle of each color 2" wide, 4" long for the medium value pieces.

Cut a rectangle of each color 1" wide, 4" long for the lighter value pieces and mix it with an equal amount of white or off-white clay.

Cut a rectangle of each color 1¾" wide, 4" long for the darker value pieces and mix it with a ¼" wide, 4" long strip of black clay. (Adjust colors as desired.)

Cut all of these colors into 2" wide, 4" long rectangles. Do <u>not</u> back these with black, yet.

Roll six sheets of conditioned **Black** clay, 5½" wide on the <u>thinnest</u> setting possible, at least 4" long. These will provide visual color separation by placing a color rectangle on the black clay and trimming the black to fit.

See *Chapter 3 – Color*

65

Assembling the Sunshine & Shadows Cane

All of the pieces in the cane are ⅛" square strips, 4" long. To back only the clay which will actually be used for the strips, use the pattern and the layout shown below to determine the width of the rectangle you will need for each color. Cut the rectangle from each color, back it with the thin sheet of black. Then cut the number of strips shown for each color.

Dark Red – 2" wide rectangle, 16 strips

Mid Red – 1½" wide rectangle, 12 strips

Light Red – 1½" wide rectangle, 12 strips

Dark Teal – 1" wide rectangle, 8 strips

Mid Teal – ½" wide rectangle, 4 strips

Light Teal – 1½" wide rectangle, 12 strips

Dark Green – ½" wide rectangle, 4 strips

Mid Green – 1" wide rectangle, 8 strips

Light Green – ¼" wide rectangle, 1 strip

Keep these strips easily accessible in color groups. Rotate the strips a quarter turn with the black edges all facing the same side.

Arrange the strips into rows carefully following the pattern and the layout shown below.

Assemble the strips into rows by sliding each strip into place using a firm straight-edge tool. Compress each row side-to-side without changing its size.

Place one side of each row on a thin sheet of black clay. Trim to fit.

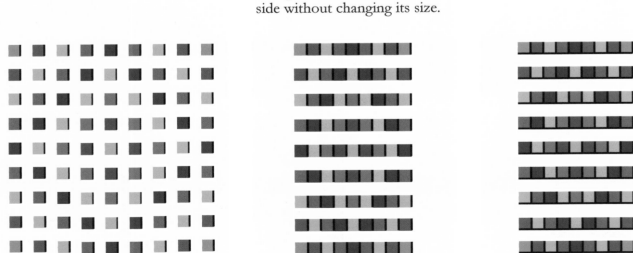

Finishing the Sunshine & Shadows Quilt Cane

Stack the nine rows together carefully matching the corners. Compress the cane slightly.

Place the two sides of the cane that are not already lined with black on a thin sheet of black clay and cut to fit.

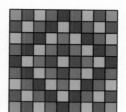

Roll a sheet of clay in one of the border colors on a medium setting. Place each side of the cane on this clay and cut to fit. Reduce as desired.

Assembling the Sunshine & Shadows Quilt Cane in Quadrants

This option for assembling a Sunshine & Shadow cane requires very careful reduction and assembly. The reward is cutting larger strips that are easier to handle for the initial cane. It also requires only 21 strips instead of 81. The initial strips are cut from double thicknesses of the color rectangles in ¼" widths.

Assemble a corner of the cane as four rows of five colors. It will be 1" by 1¼" and 4" long.

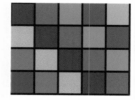

Place the long side of the cane that is not already lined with black on a sheet of thin black clay and cut to fit.

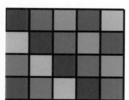

Reduce this cane to ½" by 5/8", about 16" long.

Cut a single strip of clay in the center color 1/8" square, 4" long. Do not back with black.

Cut the cane into four 4" long segments. Carefully position the segments as shown below. Center the center strip.

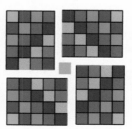

Assemble these pieces into a single cane. It should look just like the cane assembled from 81 individual pieces.

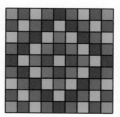

A Group Project

The diagrams shown below are for a much larger cane using the same colors as shown in the guidelines. The cane is 17 rows of 17 strips (289 pieces). This is an interesting project to complete as a group and produces a cane large enough to share among seven to ten participants.

The colors and assembly sequence.

The finished cane bordered with one of the colors in the cane.

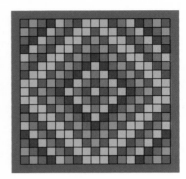

Roll sheets of conditioned clay in each color 6" long (5½" wide, ⅛" thick). For consistency, try to roll all the colors on the same pasta machine before cutting rectangles for strips. Cut rectangles at least 4¼" wide, 6" long. Extra clay can be used to wrap the finished cane segment.

Each member can initially be responsible for a single color. Mix the color, cut the rectangle, back it with a thin sheet of black, cut the strips and arrange them on an index card with the black edge facing to one side.

Arrange the sheets of strips in the assembly sequence. In this example it is: dark teal, teal, red, dark red, light red, green, dark green, light green, light teal. Each member is now responsible for assembling two rows of the cane. The first member picks up a strip of each color, starting with dark teal, through light teal, then back again through dark teal. As the first and last rows are identical, that member repeats the selection for the last row.

Move the first sheet of color strips (dark teal in this example) to the end of the line. The second member collects strips for the second and sixteenth rows, beginning and ending with light teal. This process continues through eight pairs of rows. The ninth member does only the one center row.

Each member assembles the two rows and adds the thin black clay on the bottom of the row. The most precise cane assembler in the group stacks the rows together, carefully matching the corners. The best cane reducer now reduces this 2⅛" square, 5½" long cane to 1⅛" square, over 20" long.

Cut the cane into equal segments for all members. Members can wrap the segments in different colors.

Color Variations

The color variations shown below illustrate the impact of the black separation line between colors, especially in the first pair where the color values have so little contrast. Of course, neither is wrong, it is a matter of personal preference.

In a traditional Sunshine & Shadow quilt there are very wide borders. In a polymer clay rendition the borders are narrow, emphasizing the pattern.

Almost Neon
Bright colors with a wider border, no black accent lines.

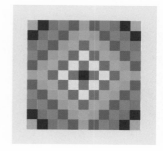

Red, Green, Blue
Three values of three colors, narrow border, no black lines.

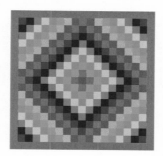

Black, White, Red, Grey
High contrast, double borders.

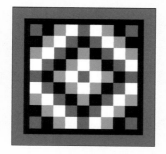

Darker Border
The same colors as above, with black accent lines.

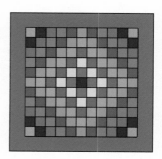

Darker Border
The same colors as above, with black accent lines.

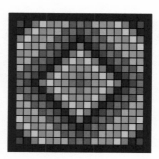

Black, White, Red, Grey
Black accent lines emphasizing contrast.

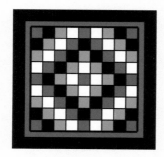

Drunkard's Path

A "Cause" Quilt

Drunkard's Path is a two color traditional quilt done in a curved pattern. The design, when made in blue and white, is associated with the Temperance Movement. It creates jagged crisscrossing diagonal lines, reminiscent of staggering home after a long night out. Other names for this pattern include Old Maid's Puzzle, Rocky Road to Kansas, Love Ring, None-Such, and World Without End.

The effectiveness of just two contrasting colors is beautifully illustrated in this quilt pattern.

Drunkard's Path is a great example of the millefiore caning technique. There is a single block pattern, made in two canes. The pattern is a blue square with a white quarter-circle in one corner, and a white square with a blue quarter-circle in one corner.

Using an extruder, the two shapes are extruded and placed together forming a square cane. Without an extruder, a round log of one color is wrapped with the other color. The sides are trimmed back to form a square. Then the cane is cut in four quadrants for the starting canes.

Two canes in each set of colors are combined in an intricate pattern for the second block cane. This second cane is again reduced and cut into four segments. These segments are assembled into the Drunkard's Path by rotating the second canes before assembly. A simple border completes the full quilt pattern.

Several interesting quilt patterns can be made from the two initial block canes. And, unlike quilting with fabric, polymer clay does not require the experienced piecing skills required to join curved edges.

Colors

See *Chapter 3 – Color*

Clay Preparation

Roll sheets of conditioned clay in two colors (5½" wide, ⅛" thick):
Blue – 10" long   **White** – 8" long

When using a polymer clay extruder, the clay must be conditioned until it is quite soft. Roll the clay into logs which fit into the extruder.

Roll a sheet of conditioned blue clay for the final cane wrap, 4" long, 5½" wide, on a medium setting.

Notice the other color choices shown in 'Variations' at the end of this section.

In the Black, White and Red pieces, one of the black quarter-circle shapes is replaced with a red quarter-circle. These logs are then placed in different positions in the second cane assembly giving two variations.

The Red, Coral and Ivory is exactly half Red with Ivory and half Coral with Ivory. They are alternated in the third cane assembly.

Also, notice the other patterns in 'Variations'. These can be easily created with leftover segments from the block cane assemblies.

Assembling the Block Canes

These canes are assembled from two shapes in two colors. One shape is a square, with a quarter-circle cut out, the other shape is the quarter-circle in the other color. The shapes can be cut from a cane as shown in these first steps.

Roll a circular log in blue clay, about 1" in diameter, about 2" long. Wrap this log with white until it is just over 2" in diameter. Cut down through the sides of the cane forming a square.

Cut down through this cane forming four quadrants as shown. Reduce each of these to ½" square canes, about 4" long.

Repeat these steps for the canes in the opposite color pair for four more canes.

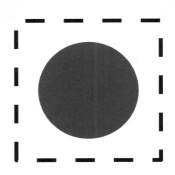

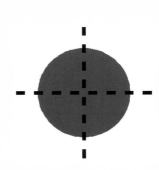

These shapes can also be formed with an extruder. Extrude about two-thirds of the white clay into the square shape. Extrude the other third into the quarter-circle shape. Cut off the excess from the longer extrusion. Extrude the same lengths in blue clay, reserving the extra blue for the final cane wraps. Assemble block canes for each color pair.

Assembling the Second and Third Canes

Reduce the block canes to about ½" square. The second cane is assembled from two segments of the block canes in each color pair. Compress these sections into a single cane. Reduce the cane if necessary until it is at least 8" long.

Cut the cane into four equal segments. Arrange these segments in a pinwheel fashion. Compress these segments into a single cane. Reduce the cane to about ¾" square, at least 8" long.

Assembling the Drunkard's Path Quilt Cane

Cut the cane into four equal segments. Compress these segments into a single cane. Reduce the cane to about ¾" square, at least 8" long.

Cut the cane into four equal segments. Compress these segments into a single cane. Place each side of the cane on a sheet of blue clay rolled on a medium setting, cut to fit. Reduce the finished cane to about 1½" square.

Variations

Fewer Blocks
This intensifies the individual elements.

Black, White, Red
Two arrangements from identical block cane sets.

Bits and Pieces
These use the initial block cane color pairs.

Monochromatic
Adding a mid-range color value softens the overall pattern

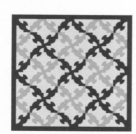

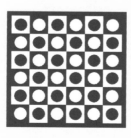

Tumbling Blocks

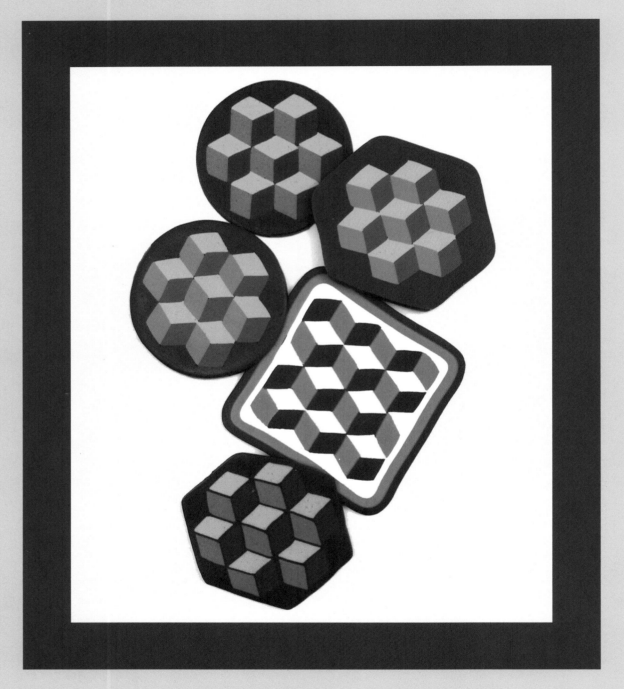

An Optical Illusion

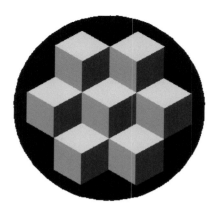

Tumbling Blocks quilt patterns have an intriguing interplay of color and dimension. The illusion of stacked cubes is achieved with a single diamond shape and varying intensities of colors. The diamonds are arranged in a hexagon formation with the light, medium and dark diamonds used in the same positions throughout the quilt.

Also known as **Baby Blocks**, this is one of the best known mosaic, or one-shape, designs. This quilt is often completed with at most a narrow border.

Creating the **Tumbling Blocks** pattern in a polymer clay cane is done with diamond shaped logs. Extruding these diamond shapes is the easiest and most straightforward process. The die for this diamond shape is the one with a 60° angle at the point. The diamond shape can also be formed from two equilateral triangular logs, either hand formed or extruded. The triangular logs are placed back to back to form the diamond.

For the cane shown above and in the guidelines, three diamond shapes in contrasting colors are assembled into a hexagonal shaped cane. If the starting diamond shapes are quite large, this cane may need to be carefully reduced. Seven of the hexagon cane segments are then placed together to form the Tumbling Blocks pattern.

To complete the cane, six diamond shaped logs are formed with black clay and inserted around the Tumbling Blocks patterns. This forms a larger hexagon shape. This is then wrapped on all sides with strips of black clay.

If desired, the cane can be carefully reduced while maintaining the hexagon shape. Slices of the cane can be left as hexagons or can be trimmed into a circular shape using a circle cutter.

Colors

See Chapter 3 – Color

Clay Preparation

Roll sheets of conditioned clay in four colors (5½" wide, ⅛" thick):
> **Pale Gold** – 4" long
> **Gold** – 4" long
> **Brick Red** – 4" long
> **Black** – 8" long

Keep half of the sheet of black clay for wrapping the finished canes.

Prepare the rest of the clay for an extruder or hand formed logs.

When using a polymer clay extruder, the clay must be conditioned until it is quite soft. Roll the clay into logs which will fit into an extruder.

Without an extruder, the clay will be shaped into triangular logs which will then be formed into diamond shaped logs.

Forming the Tumbling Blocks Diamonds

Three diamond shaped logs are assembled into each Tumbling Block. If the starting diamond shaped logs are quite large, the block cane will be reduced.

Without a diamond shaped extruder die, form or extrude two triangular shaped logs in each of three contrasting colors and black. Form these into diamond shaped logs.

Or, extrude diamond shaped logs in three contrasting colors and black using a 60° diamond die.

Assembling a Tumbling Block Cane

Assemble the three color diamond shaped logs into a hexagonal shaped cane. Reduce this cane if it is large or make several block canes from smaller diamond shaped logs.

Place seven of the hexagon cane segments together to form the tumbling blocks pattern.

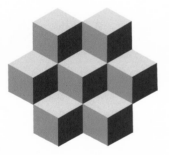

Place six of the black diamond shaped logs around the sides to form a hexagon shaped cane.

Place each side of the cane on a sheet of black clay and trim it to fit. Reduce if desired.

To make the circular shape, take a slice from the hexagon shaped cane. Carefully position a circle cutter over the pattern and cut away the edge.

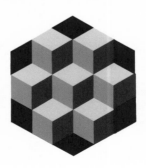

Assembling a Tumbling Blocks Quilt Cane

The Tumbling Block canes can also be assembled into a cane representing a full quilt. This will use several block canes. There are 22 cane segments shown in the example.

Place block cane segments in this pattern with the same orientation. The lightest color on top, darkest on the bottom to one side, mid-range on the bottom to the other side. Trim away the sides of the cane to a square.

The finished cane can be wrapped with a thin sheet of black clay. It can be further reduced without losing detail.

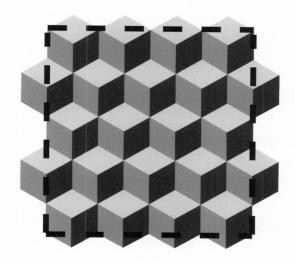

Variations

Black, White, Red
Placed in a dark grey background.

Shades of Greys
In a black background.

Black, White, Red
In a full quilt cane.

6. Print Design Variations

In addition to the geometric shapes that go into the preceding quilt pattern canes, there are many other kinds of design elements. The wide range of prints found in textiles is easy to recreate in polymer clay. These canes can be used in many ways, including as components in building very intricate canes. Nine-Patch quilts made with square cane components using **Florals, Stripes, Polka Dots** and more lend charm and variety to the design. Any simple cane can be cut apart and recombined to create the kind of repeats found in textiles.

Canes styles such as **Linoleum** and **Lace** can be used as backgrounds in more complex canes or by themselves as a print. Square repeat canes allow for easy creation of smaller scale staggered designs and can be cut and placed on a backing to form sheets of clay fabric.

When formed into triangle and square components, even random but colorful designs can be recombined to form more regular mirrored repeats. **Kaleidoscope** canes are made in this manner.

These are examples of kaleidoscope canes by Shane Smith. She takes cane components like the white and purple pieces shown at left and reduces, combines, morphs and recombines to create intricate patterns as seen here.

Floral Canes

To make a floral cane, you will usually need a center, petals and perhaps a leaf or two. Centers can be a simple snake or bulls-eye, or a grouping of them; spirals (jellyrolls) make great centers for roses. Petals can be fat and rounded, long and thin, in single rows or layers.

Make them a solid color or shaded in either horizontal or vertical ways.

Horizontal shading is achieved by stacking layers of progressively lighter or darker shades of a color in sheets. Or, take a Skinner Blend sheet and fold it accordion-style so that the dark part is on one end and the light on the other end of the resulting folded stack. A Skinner Blend sheet can also be made into a jelly-roll so that the dark part is either in the center or the outside as you choose.

   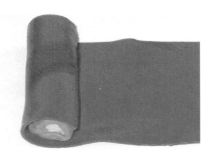

This cane is about 3" across and 4" tall when built. It has petals made from an accordion folded Skinner Blend made using purple, blue and white. The center is a yellow bulls-eye wrapped in orange and then in red. Flower canes are the perfect place to relax and try new things and to practice reduction. A little distortion does not show nearly as much on florals as it does on stripes and geometric shapes.

The leaf also begins as a Skinner Blend, but with only a slight variation from darker to lighter green. Rolled up, it shades from dark in the center to lighter outside. Slice down the entire length and line with a thin sheet of black to form the vein. Realign the leaf parts and point the top and bottom by squeezing. The remaining green is rolled into a sheet and placed on a thin sheet of black, and then rolled up to form a slight jellyroll. This will be a tendril in the flower.

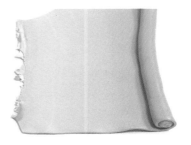 

Petals are placed around the center and leaf sections are placed in between.

Two sections of tendrils help fill in space as well, then white snakes fill in to bring the shape to a squared off plug shape.

Carefully reduced, this can then be cut in sections and recombined. This gives a grid or even repeat effect. Starting with a vivid flower allows for a great deal of reduction and still the details can be seen.

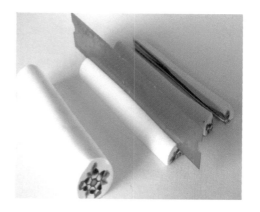

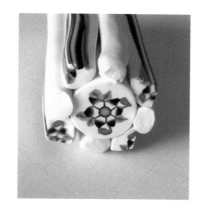

The original cane can also be reduced to a round cane instead of a square. Just morph the corners inward, and as the background is solid white, no distortion is visible. All round canes can be used to create staggered repeats by using this handy technique.

Start with two equal lengths of cane. Cut one section down the center into half round cane sections, and then cut each half round into quarters as shown.

Place the quarter sections around the remaining round cane section as shown, points facing outward and with a space in between each; these will be the new corners. Fill in the spaces with white snakes. This can be used as a square in a Nine Patch, or reduced and recombined.

This same technique is used with a green and white bulls-eye. After quartering and placing the quarters point side out, fill with white and reduce. Recombine several times to reduce to polka dots.

Square canes can be cut into triangles or other shapes and recombined as quilt blocks using two or more different patterns.

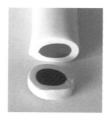

Linoleum Canes have bits of color that float in a jumbled way reminiscent of floor tiles. This is an excellent way to use scraps and ends from cane making.

Chop cane scraps or two or more colors of conditioned clay. Roll pieces into a snake, reduce and recombine. The more they are recombined, the tighter the effect.

Many florals and print patterns are possible to create using polymer clay. Start with enough of a strongly graphic cane, and you can recombine it in many ways. Reducing the image changes things quite a bit. So does adding a quarter from another cane at the corners, or packing with a color different from the background. Always try to cut a length to keep from each section before you change it drastically, and then you will have a selection of different scales and styles.

Lace Canes can be made using any simple or complex pattern while restricting the color choices to white, off-white, and translucent. Premo!™ translucent with bleach, also know as Premo!™ color Frost, darkens the least of the translucent clays, and is very effective here.

It can also be used as background in floral canes, and when sliced very thin and applied, both lace canes and floral canes made with translucent make use of an optical illusion. The translucent quietly disappears from view, allowing a layered or dimensional floating effect. Also, when pieces made using canes with translucent are sanded and buffed, they become very glassy with no glaze needed.

Leigh Ross is a master of these canes. Her lace canes were used on the book cover, the table of contents and are shown at right.

Her floral canes are often quite vivid whereas the lace canes are ghostly pale and delicate.

Kaleidoscope canes refer to those canes made into sections of three, four, five or more and recombined with mirrored sections. Sandra McCaw uses stacks of clay in graduated colors at least five sheets high. Angled cuts through these stacked loaves form wedges. Wedges are combined in different ways to form a square. The square is morphed so that the corners are now the sides and the former sides become corners.

When cut into quarters and recombined, these form amazing patterns. Sandra combines, recombines and reduces her canes to a fantastic degree. If you want to learn how she does it, get her video, *The McCaw Cane,* abba dabba Productions. (See *Chapter 11 – Sources*). Even forgetting some parts and changing others when trying her technique turned out just fine and the patterns are hypnotically fun to create. There really are no mistakes in polymer clay. There are just new techniques and variations.

Cane slices can be applied to a backing piece of clay or used alone to create buttons and earrings.

Many uncured cane slices can be applied to a flat sheet of raw polymer clay to create a fabric look.

This can be cut and used to cover things like needle cases, thimbles, box lids, switch plate covers, eggs and just about anything that can withstand baking at near 300° F in the oven.

84

7. Surface Applications

Carolyn Potter

Now that you have made millefiore canes, the question becomes "What can I do with them?".

Carolyn Potter creates her Goddess Figures and then covers them with cane slices. She bakes at several stages to allow for handling the clay without deforming the canes. The figure seen at left features Log Cabin quilt block patterns as well as many others.

You can also cover small pieces of clay with cane slices and roll them to create beads. These can be pierced before baking or drilled afterwards.

Use a hand drill or a small leather hole punch like the one made by BeadSmith to easily create small holes in baked slices. With a jump ring or some wire wrapping, you can make charms and dangles for jewelry use.

Button backs (shanks) in metal and acrylic forms can be purchased from suppliers of jewelry components and findings like Rio Grande or Fire Mountain Gems. Post and clip-on earring backs are available as well. These can simply be glued to baked cane slices using TiteBond™ or a superglue of your choice. (See *Chapter 11 – Sources).*

Better yet, bake the metal backs in place. Use a Kemper cutter and a thin sheet of clay that coordinates with your cane slices to make small circles slightly larger than your shank or post finding. You can also make them large enough to show behind your tile. Button shanks require making a second smaller hole in the center of the circle, then placing it neatly through the hole. The earring posts can be poked through by themselves.

Place a small dot of liquid clay where you wish to place the finding, then add the finding and circle. Press the circle gently into place to seal and re-bake.

Canes can also be used to create a kind of "fabric" that can be used to cover metal, wood, or paper items and even blown eggs.

When slicing canes, make them as even as possible. Use a very sharp blade. Roll out a sheet of backing clay at a medium thickness and carefully place the canes on it. Put them next to each other, or stagger the rows. You can even use more than one kind of cane if you choose.

Lightly press them all into place, smooth with the acrylic rod roller, and use the pasta machine set at the widest opening. Designs will stretch when being rolled again at smaller settings, so be sure to set the opening back to the widest setting and decrease gradually as desired.

A cookie cutter or paper pattern makes it easy to get exactly the right piece when covering items although you can also ease to fit. Just be careful not to stretch too much or the design will distort. Make templates for items you cover repeatedly.

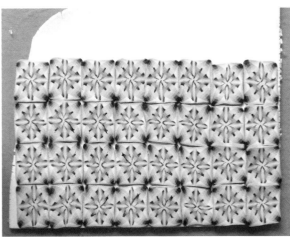

Cover the items and re-bake. Support pieces and keep them from touching the baking surface by using polyester fiberfill stuffing. At the correct baking temperatures, it will not melt.

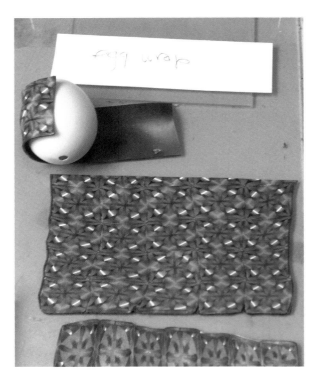

Decorate a Sewing Kit

Cover a standard metal thimble with clay, and press lightly into place.

Cover a wooden needle case with a rectangle of clay cut to size on the sides and a circle on the bottom using a Kemper cutter. Do not cover the top of the neck that fits in the cap.

Cover the cap with a strip cut to fit and a circle. Meld seams lightly with pressure.

The pin box is made from a recycled candy tin. The box was painted with several coats of water based paint which can be baked at low temperatures. If using spray paints or enamels, <u>do not</u> bake the paints. Glue a baked circle in place with superglue as the last step when using these paints.

A circle shaped cutter was used to fill the indentation already in the lid and the 'Press' area was cut away with a craft knife.

After baking the tin may be lined with felt if desired. Spray adhesive applied to the felt is the best way to attach it to the inside of the box.

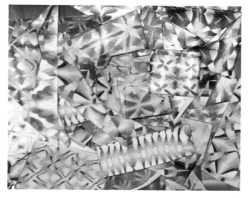

As every quilter knows always save your scraps. The bits shown at left have been baked, and can be used as a mosaic tile on other surfaces. Baked pieces can be cut to fit with scissors and applied with glues like E6000™.

Another way to use cane slices is to apply them to textured surfaces. In the example at right, a rubber stamp was used to impress the clay. Gold acrylic paint was applied to the recesses and wiped from the surface.

Slices of cane were applied after removing the excess translucent wrap clay using a small star shaped cutter's points. When smoothed into place during application to a surface, the canes meld with barely visible seams.

Textures and Tiles

A release agent is often used with texturing pieces, molds and stamps. Some artists prefer talcum powder or cornstarch. Water sprayed lightly from a small misting bottle works well when used with rubber and plastic textures.

Unmounted stamps, Shadex™ texture sheets and coarse wet/dry sandpaper can all be put through the pasta machine right along with the clay.

Roll out a sheet of conditioned clay to a medium thickness. Set the pasta machine back to the widest opening. Lightly mist the stamp or texture sheet, and hold next to the clay sheet. Do not try to attach it as it will move when in the machine.

Put both pieces through the machine together and catch them as they come out. The machine pressure is far superior to what you can get with a hand roller.

When using a hand roller, apply the clay to the texture surface and press the clay down with the roller, rather than applying the surface to the clay and pressing the texture surface with the roller.

The faux fabric bolts shown below were made using Shadex™ texture sheets and clay in this manner. Pearl-Ex™ powders were carefully applied to the raised surfaces with a fingertip. After powders or inks are applied to raised surfaces, clay can be put through the pasta machine again or gently hand rolled to flatten raised surfaces if desired. This can mimic brocade textiles and metallic or iridescent prints.

Wipe the rollers after use with powders or inks. Use a paper towel, cloth or baby-wipe.

Bryan Helm

Shape cutters can be used on scraps as work progresses on any project. Build up a supply of mosaic tiles to use on larger pieces. This guitar is tiled in a Tumbling Blocks quilt pattern

Margie Drake

Ready Stamps

Rubber stamps are a wonderful source of impression designs for use with clay, as well as being useful for applying inks or powders.　However, commercially available stamps have limitations when being used to produce items you mean to sell.

If you want to use designs freely, you can have rubber stamps and molds (called matrix trays and used in forming the rubber sheets) made through Ready Stamps. You can get uncut sheets of rubber stamps made to your original designs or with copyright-free designs.　There are hundreds of books with thousands of images in many styles.

If you specifically ask when ordering, you can also get the plate and matrix tray included with your unmounted sheet of stamps. You can order a sheet of designs that measures nine inches by seven inches. Send in the black and white high contrast artwork along with payment (less than $40 at this time) and within weeks you will have a set of tools that include the unmounted rubber sheet and the matrix tray. This is a polymer board that is the 'in-ny' version of all the designs, while the rubber stamps are the 'out-ties'. Matrix trays can be used to create buttons and tiles or to create textured sheets of clay.

You start with the artwork. All the black areas in your design will be raised on the stamps. You can use original drawings in pen and ink, computer graphic printouts or photocopies. This allows you to play with scale as well. Reducing or enlarging designs can make quite a difference in the overall design. With a computer, you have access to a overwhelming amount of choices in fonts and images that are copyright-free and their potential variations in use.

In a dingbat, or 'ornamental' font, each letter and character on the keyboard can be used to represent a design, so that that image appears when you type the corresponding letter. There are thousands of dingbat fonts available for download on the Internet. Some are already included with the set of fonts that come installed in computers with your software. Many of the designer fonts available are 'shareware' or 'freeware', meaning that anyone can use the images freely by permission of the designer at little or no cost. Other fonts must be purchased in order to use them for commercial purposes. Many fonts will come in a .zip file that contains the font (.ttf) file itself plus information about the artist and the conditions of use. It is important to respect the copyrights of all artists and authors, and to give credit where credit is due.

A favorite dingbat font is an interlocking set called 'Quilters Delight' that was designed by Gabrielle Gaither, and her condition for commercial use was $5 and name credit. (It costs $2.00 for non-commercial use.) A font called Amish Quilts was used to create graphics for the Miniature Textile Shoppe seen in *Chapter 8 – "Pieces"*.

For more information on using dingbat fonts and Ready Stamps, visit www.polyclay.com/ready.htm

Hawaiian Quilt Tops

Another set of dingbat fonts is called Hawaiian Quilts 1, 2 and 3, and it can be found at www.actionfonts.com It effectively captures the very graphic look of this style of quilt top. The characters shown at right are only a few of the dozens in this set. The letters represented here are: a, c, d, e, f and k, l, y, z, b.

Adobe Photoshop™ is a useful program allowing manipulation of size, color and the option of layers that include drop shadows, outlines and more. This is not important in making rubber stamp designs, but almost essential when creating transfers with liquid clay.

When the resulting images are are printed on photographic paper (particularly Epson Glossy Photo Paper™) the ink can be transferred to liquid clays or to sheets of solid uncured clay.

Leave some area outside the design and cut out as desired. Brush the liquid clay onto the cut print in a thin even layer. Place on a baking tile and allow to settle for a few minutes. Poke any air bubbles you see with a pin, but the liquids will self-level fairly well. Bake according to manufacturer's directions.

After baking, the transfered image can be peeled easily from the photo paper. Other brands do not work as well, and the piece must be soaked in water and rubbed gently to remove any paper backing that sticks.

Many artists also use T-shirt transfer paper or Lazertrans™, but Epson Glossy Photo Paper™ is our brand of choice.

The cured transfer is a fairly sturdy sheet of translucent plastic with many possible uses. It can be sewn, glued or put into further assemblies and re-baked. A film of the liquid applied to the transfer's back with a makeup sponge is helpful in affixing it to sheets of raw clay.

Another way to use these fonts with Adobe Photoshop™ or other graphic editing programs is to create your own cards, calendars and more. Images can be layered to great effect, just as appliqué is done with fabric. Instead of needle and thread, the images can be placed on top of each other inside the computer itself. Borders or backgrounds can be added.

By using polymer clay images as a background layer, images such as these can be created easily. Print them out on glossy photo paper to make your own greeting cards, or upload images to Print On Demand businesses like Cafepress or Lulu. They will print the image on cards, calendars, coffee mugs, T-shirts and much more. Use them as gifts or as an effective and low cost way to advertise your artwork.

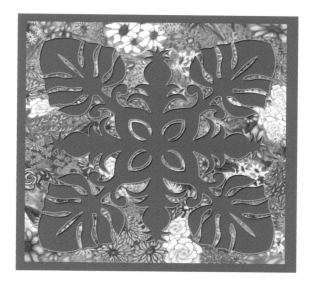

The four designs seen here are the letters e, f, s and y placed on top of polymer clay tiles created by Leigh Ross. This placement is done with the computer, but it could be done with actual clay transfers as well.

See the tiles by themselves in *Chapter 9 – Gallery.*

Each letter has layer styles added including drop shadow, inner shadow, and inner and outer highlights. These effects help give the illusion of a stitched appliqué quilt top.

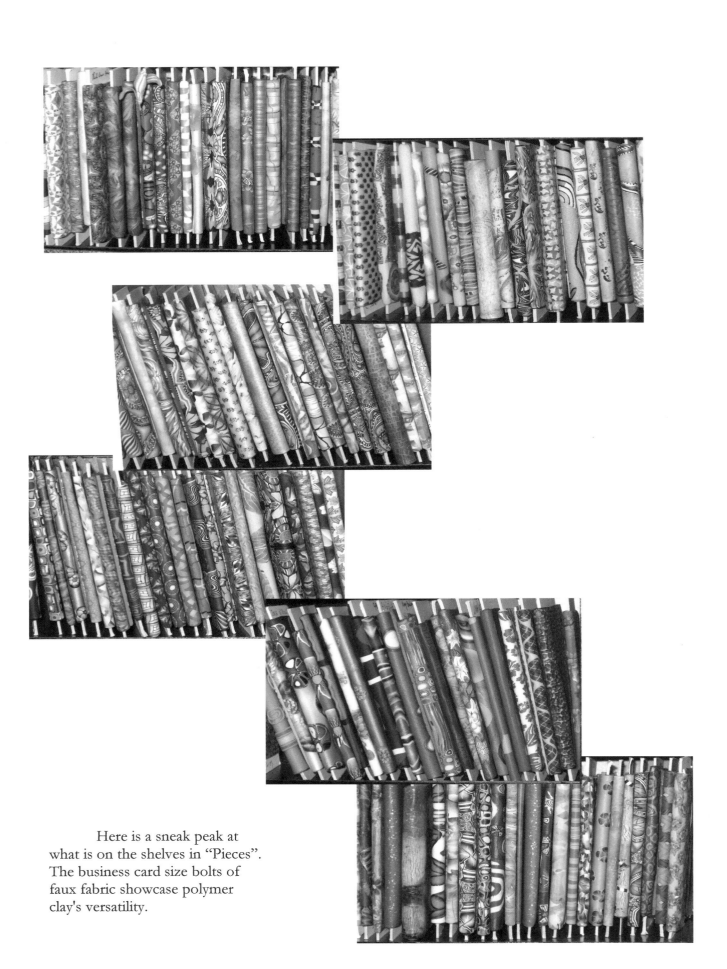

Here is a sneak peak at what is on the shelves in "Pieces". The business card size bolts of faux fabric showcase polymer clay's versatility.

8. "Pieces"
The Miniature Textile Shoppe

When I was a little girl, my mother would take me with her to shop for fabrics. A skilled and also practical seamstress, she usually had specific garments or projects in mind. I would wander freely amidst the bolts and notions, with no particular ideas in mind but an imagination that far surpassed any knowledge or skills I had at that time. Oh, the remembered delights that could be found there! An overwhelming display of color and pattern to feed the eyes and stimulate the mind, and the additional sensory delights of texture and touch were also profound. Silks, satins, velvets...crisp cottons, smooth polyesters, seersucker's puckers and corduroy's rows; all available to be touched by little girls (and grownup seamstresses!) with clean fingers. Projects sprang effortlessly to mind when gazing at the rows of shelves with the colors so vibrantly displayed!

Decades later, that sense of wonder and possibility has never faded for me. Fabric stores have been joined by outlets for all sorts of craft materials, and I still find great joy in wandering the aisles, in finding new sources for textiles and trims and notions.

One of the first things that came to my mind when this book was first proposed was "Quilts in Polymer Clay... now, wouldn't it be wonderful to have a little polymer clay fabric store too?". Little, because another long-term love for me is miniatures. I am fascinated by scale models and have always enjoyed making things for my dolls. I still do! I envisioned a room full of bolts of faux fabrics made of polymer clay. I could see the floor laid in black and white tiles, in a quilt pattern, of course. I had lots of canes already made and waiting to be used, and suddenly it all seemed to me as though it could really be done. And so I began to put together this little store, "Pieces" – The Miniature Textile Shoppe.

I found a dingbat font called Amish Quilts and when I saw this particular image, I knew I had the start of the floor tile plan. The font was used in making both the store bags and sign.

"Pieces" started out much like a stage set model. A 2' by 4' piece of Styrofoam™ insulation foam was cut to fit the table on which it was built. Hot wire cutters and foam are a good way to create shaped bases for applying mosaic work as well. Make sure to have good ventilation and never put foam in an oven. Use glue to affix baked clay. Foam board in white and a soft speckled gray were used to make the walls, and duct taped in place.

The ¾" square tiles are attached to the floor with white PVA glue. It took more than 2000 tiles to create the floor and many hours of gluing.

As I was not content with using only black and white, many shades and tones were used, ultimately making a very realistic marble tile floor in miniature.

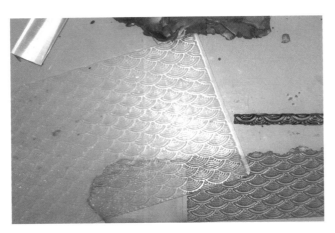

A Shadex™ texture sheet was used to form trim for the shelves and cases. Gold and black clay mixed together mimics a lovely aged wood color.

After baking, trim pieces were stained with a mixture of Varathane™ and black acrylic paint. This is applied with a brush and wiped off of the raised surface areas, giving an antiqued effect.

Beads with stamped clay around them become feet for the showcases, and medallions that appear to be carved are actually bits of clay pressed into matrix tray molds from Ready Stamps™.

The large shelves in the store are made of foam board and spray painted black. The cutting table is made the same way. Trim made of polymer clay was glued into place.

The double cases are created from processed cheese boxes that are stacked two high and painted with acrylic paint in a mix of gold and black.

Baked polymer clay trim was applied to some areas, and the boxes were lined with paper. Faux marble tops were made by barely mixing white clay with tiny amounts of black and gold clays.

Now the store has its basics – a table, some counters and shelves. Tiny books on quilting and polymer clay are made with cut out pictures from a catalog from F&W Publications with their permission.

It is time for fabric. Lots of fabric! I made small bolts of solid colors using clays I had on hand. For variety, translucent clays were mixed with embossing powders for interesting effects that were still largely solid colors.

I soon realized I was going to need some assistance. I put out the call to our wonderful friends who attend the annual polymer clay guild retreat here in Colorado. Traditionally, quilters will help each other; sharing their favorite fabrics, sharing the labor, their time and their knowledge freely within circles of friends. So it was to be within the polymer clay circle. Not only did the artists from Internet newsgroups like Polymer Clay Central and my local guild respond, but others from across America did as well.

Lindly Haunani bravely volunteered to take the matte board bolt inserts and instructions with her to Shrinemont, the National Polymer Clay Guild annual event. All the artists who participated took their 3" by 5" sheets of decorated polymer clay and wrapped them around the business card sized matte board pieces to become bolts of faux fabric.

Whether they created one bolt or a collection, each artist made a unique contribution to this project. What went far beyond my early expectations was the range and scope of the various bolts. No two are alike. All are wonderful! As the collection grew, so did my feeling of connection to all the people who participated.

The box of bolts that Lindly mailed to me from Shrinemont weighed over six pounds. That is a lot of clay bolts.

As it turned out, the contributing artists all saved the day. I did not have as much time to fill the shelves as I had hoped, and these dear people helped do it for me.

Each individual bolt is fabulous in its own way. Each is a representation of a different way to use polymer clay. Some are stamped, many are caned, some have large design elements, some small. They all vary beautifully as do full scale textiles. Thanks to all who helped make it happen.

These are just a few of the bolts in this collection. Artists include Rita Sharon, Melanie West, Karen Wentink, and Marla Frankenberg.

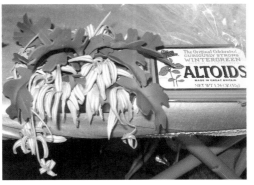

Because I had so much assistance in creating the fabric, I was able to add some details like the plants on the tops of the shelves. These tiny spider plants are made using a Skinner Blend to create a leaf cane, which is then individually cut and formed to make each plant. The candy box shows the actual size of this "planter box". Details are important to the overall effect of a scale model or a full-sized store.

Quilt canes made by Judith Skinner decorate the walls of this miniature textile shoppe. Any 11½" fashion doll would love to look at all the fabrics and wonderful bits found here at "Pieces".

The tape measure is also made of polymer clay. I created an image of a yellow tape measure segment and reduced it using Photoshop™. Then Fimo™ Gel, one of the liquid clays, was used to create a transfer, and that is what you see here.

Even full sized patrons have a fabulous time rearranging the collection and putting the bolts together in different ways. While only a fraction of each design is visible here in the little store, all contribute to a marvelous set.

Both textile and polymer clay artists collect ideas and inspirations, tools and materials. What quilter does not have a stash of unfinished quilts? What polymer clay artist does not have a shelf of unfinished pieces? Projects for another day are all part of the scheme of things for artists.

That is the secret of good quilts and of good friendships too. Both will help keep you warm and content when the world seems cold.

9. Gallery

Patti Weber

Margie Drake

Dede Leupold

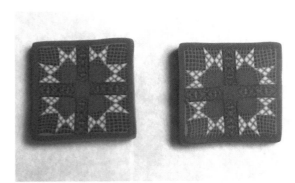

Dede Leupold

Laura Humenek

Jenny Patterson

Dede Leupold

Karen Woods

Sharon Ohlhorst

Jenny Patterson

Sharon Olhorst

Dede Leupold

Karen Woods

Barb Fajardo

Barb Fajardo

Karen Woods

100

Katerina Musetti   *photo: Richard A. Stoner*

Jenny Patterson

Karen Woods

Jenny Patterson

All photographs in the gallery section are provided by the authors or the artists unless otherwise noted in the caption.

Karen Woods

Jenny Patterson

Jenny Patterson

Karen Woods

Jenny Patterson

102

Violette Laporte

Natalia Garcia deLeaniz

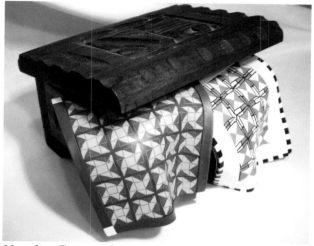

Natalia Garcia deLeaniz

Natalia Garcia deLeaniz

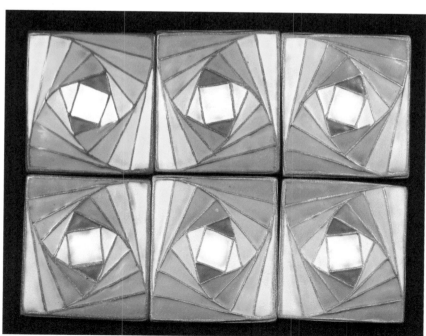

Violette Laporte

Lisa Clarke

Violette Laporte

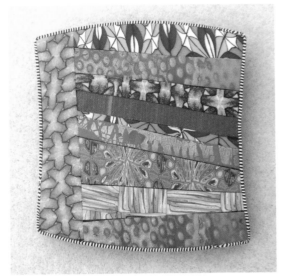

Francie Owens

Pat Sernyk

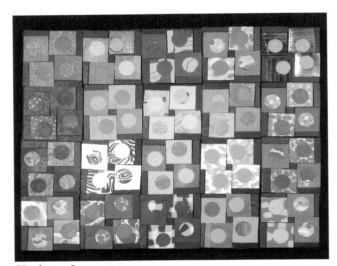

Violette Laporte

Linda Hess

Layl McDill

Katerina Musetti   photo: Richard A. Stoner

Sharon Ohlhorst

Francie Owens

Sharon Ohlhorst

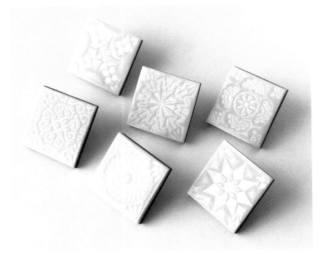

Melanie West

Melanie West

Shirley Rufener (detail from below)

Melanie West

Linda Hess

Shirley Rufener

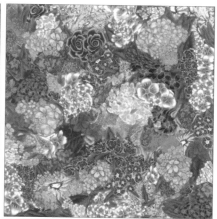

Leigh Ross

Rachel Tirosh

Karen Swiech
photo Tim Henderson

Karen Woods

Bryan Helm

10. Artist Information

We are nourished by a long tradition of women working together to make beautiful, complex works of art that would be otherwise almost impossible to accomplish alone. The Quilting Bee is a time honored blend of industry and conviviality, where more than just the work is shared freely within the group.

Friendship Quilts are a lasting material memento of the generosity and warmth that unite these widespread circles of sisters and friends. We feel strongly that this book is our own version of such a quilt, with each part given to us by wonderful people who have enriched our personal experience and this book.

Thank you!

Bette Abdu
www.abbadabbavideo.com

Oscelyn Anderson
www.whimsicalclaycreations.com

Richard Bassett
richard4clay@aol.com

Cynthia Becker
cynipid@comcast.net

Judy Belcher
jsbel@msn.com

Jana Roberts Benzon
www.janarobertsbenzon.com

AllisonBolm
www.byallison.com

Mags Bonham
mags@vtcrafts.net

Anna Bowers
wcannie@alltel.net

Eireen & Debby Brams
david.garner2@comcast.net

Jeannie Campbell
jeanbob@ptd.net

Kim Cavender
www.kimcavender.com

Lisa Clarke
www.polkadotcreations.com

Terry Lee Czechowski
tlc@tlc-creation.com

Ann Dillon
www.anndillon.com

Dayle Doroshow
dayledoroshow@hotmail.com

Margie Drake
www.madmargie.com

Barbara Fajardo
www.rubarbdesertdesigns.com

Marla Frankenberg
marlafrankenberg@comcast.net

Emi Fukushima
www.creationsbyemi.com

Natalia Garcia deLeaniz
ngleaniz@yahoo.es

Sue Gentry
cactusblum@aol.com

Kathy Gregson
gregson@erols.com

Arlene Groch
info@polymarketpress.com

Barb Harper
flyinbarb@aol.com

Lindly Haunani
www.lindlyhaunani.com

Sarajane & Bryan Helm
www.polyclay.com

Linda Hess
polymercreations4u@msn.com

Peggy Houchin
houchin00@lpbroadband.net

Ruth Ann Husted
info@polymarketpress.com

Laura Humenek
info@polymarketpress.com

Lenora Kandiner
kandiner@starlinx.com

Jeanette Kandray
jkandray@columbus.rr.com

Donna Kato
www.katopolyclay.com

Susan Kelsey
skel@comcast.net

Hazel Keyes
claychic1@yahoo.com

Kim Korringa
www.kimcreates.com

Barbara Kunkel
studiobaku@comcast.net

Violette Laporte
fxvio@sympatico.ca

Marcia Laska
info@polymarketpress.com

Dede Leupold
bumblebeads@hotmail.com

Eileen Loring
ejloring@comcast.net

Diane Luftig
polymerdesignsbydiane.com

Layl McDill
www.claysquared.com

Carol Simmons

Diana McNamee
artsydiana@hotmail.com

Janet Miller
milljamar@hotmail.com

Holly Mion
hmion@insight.rr.com

Joyce Miskowitz
joysjewlzetc@comcast.net

Sue Mueller
suemuellersmail@aol.com

Katerina Musetti
kmusetti@libcom.com

Mari O'Dell
juanymari@aol.com

Sharon Ohlhorst
sohlhorst@weber.edu

Nancy Osbahr
ckhearts@frii.com

Francie Owens
www.francieos.com

Jennifer Patterson
www.quiltedinclay.com

Carolyn Potter
info@polymarketpress.com

Laurie Prophater
ornamental@prodigy.net

Leigh Ross
www.polymerclaycentral.com

Shirley Rufener
srufener@verizon.net

Georgia Sargeant
info@polymarketpress.com

Karen Scudder
downtowncs@aol.com

Marie Segal
www.clayfactoryinc.com

Pat Sernyk
fishwife@mts.net

Karen Sexton
bobwire123@msn.com

Amy Seymour
atseymour@hotmail.com

Rita Sharon
ritasharon8@cs.com

Sarah Shriver
www.sarahshriver.com

Cindy Silas
cindysilas@comcast.net

Jana Roberts Benzon

110

Carol Simmons
csim@frii.com

Judith Skinner
www.judithskinner.com

Shane Smith
shaneangel@aol.com

Heidi Spicer
beadcr@netzero.com

Jackie Swartz
ljcswartz@hotmail.com

Karen Swiech
kswiech@verizon.net

C.A. Therien
catherien@hotmail.com

Gayle Thompson
www.got-clay.com

Susan Tilt
susantilt@mac.com

Cynthia Tinapple
www.polymerclaydaily.com

Rachel Tirosh
rachelsart@intrater.net

Angela Tompkins
fatompkins@webtv.net

Dedra True-Scheib
DedraTS@aol.com

Sandie Weatherford
vlady6@msn.com

Patti Weber
www.beadlounge.com

Syd Wellman
polymuse@comcast.net

Linda Wentink
info@polymarketpress.com

Melanie West
www.melanieweststudio.com

Karen Woods
karenwoods.home.mindspring.com

Wilma Yost
www.polymerclayexpress.com

Dayle Doroshow

11. Sources

abbadabba Productions, LLC
713 Blake Hill Rd.
New Hampton NH 03256
877-744-0002
www.abbadabbavideo.com
instructional polymer clay videos

American Art Clay Co.
4717 W. 16th St.
Indianapolis IN 46222
800-372-1600
www.amaco.com
clays, molds, books, tools, and more

American Science & Surplus
3605 Howard St.
Skokie IL 60076
847-934-0722
www.sciplus.com
interesting selection, tools, things to cover

Bead Lounge
320 Main St.
Longmont CO 80501
303-678-9966
www.beadlounge.com
beads, findings and classes

Bradley's Plastic Bag Co.
9130 Firestone Blvd.
Downey CA 90241
800-621-7864
www.bradleybag.com
bags and shipping supplies, gloves

Cafépress
www.cafepress.com
print-on-demand merchandise

Clay Factory of Escondido
PO Box 460598
Escondido CA 92046
877-728-5739
www.clayfactoryinc.com
Premo, Cernit, Sculpey, cutters, tools, powders, more

Clearsnap, Inc
PO Box 98
Anacortes WA 98221
800-448-4862
www.clearsnap.com
ColorBox inks, stamping supplies

Clotilde, LLC
PO Box 7500
Big Sandy TX 75755-7500
800-772-2891
www.clotilde.com
tools, books, threads, notions, more

Dick Blick
P.O. Box 1267
Galesburg IL 61402
800-447-8192
www.dickblick.com
art supplies since 1911

The Design Library
91 Market St., Suite 1, Box 24
Wappingers Falls NY 12590
845-297-1035
www.design-library.com
textile design archive

Dharma Trading Co.
800-542-5227
www.dharmatrading.com
fiber art supplies, paints, inks, Pearl-Ex, dyes, blanks

Dover Publications
31 E. 2nd St.
Mineola NY 11501
516-294-7000
www.doverpublications.com
Dover Books, Dover Pictorial Archive Series, clip art, books

Dremel
4195 21st St.
Racine WI 53406
800-437-3635
www.dremel.com
tools

Eberhard Faber GmbH
Postfach 1120
Neumarkt Germany 92302
09181/43 0-0
manufacturer art supplies, FIMO

Elsie's Exquisiques
722 Lenox Ave.
Riverside CA 92504
800-742-SILK
www.elsiesgarden.com
braid, silk and vintage ribbons, trims, supplies, silk roses

Embellishment – Quilts, Inc.
7660 Woodway, Suite 550
Houston TX 77063
713-781-6864
www.quilts.com
Embellishment trade show, quilt & sewing shows

Fire Mountain Gems
28195 Redwood Hwy., Dept. 8418
Cave Junction OR 97523
800-355-2137
www.firemountaingems.com
beads, supplies, findings, more

Flax Art and Design
240 Valley Drive
Brisbane CA 94005
888-352-9278
www.flaxart.com
art supplies, gifts

I.B. Moore
648 Laco Drive
Lexington KY 40511
859-255-5501
www.ibmoore.com
buna cord, rubber O rings

Kemper Enterprises
13595 12th Street
Chino CA 91710
909-627-6191
www.kempertools.com
kemper clay gun, kemper cutters, tools

La Cuisine
323 Cameron St.
Alexandria VA 22314
800-521-1176
www.lacuisineus.com
canape/cookie cutters, molds, tools

Lulu
www.lulu.com
print-on-demand publishing

Micro Mark
340 Snyder Ave.
Berkeley Heights NJ 07922
800-225-1066
www.micromark.com
earth pigments, carving and modeling

National Polymer Clay Guild
PMB 345 1350 Beverly Rd., 115
McClean VA 22101
www.npcg.org
polymer clay organization

Off-the-Beaten-Path
6601D Royal Street
Pleasant Valley MO 64068
816-415-8827
www.cookiecutter.com
individual cutters and sets

Ornamental Resources
1427 Miner St., Box 3010
Idaho Springs CO 80452
800-876-6762
www.ornabead.com
stones, charms, beads, findings,supplies, more

OTT-LITE
1214 W. Cass St.
Tampa FL 33606
800-842-8848
www.ott-lite.com
true color lighting

Perfect Touch
24 Artesia
Conroe TX 77304
409-756-1942
www.perfect-touch.com
artist tools

Polka Dot Creations
Lisa Clarke
www.polkadotcreations.com
books and more

Polyform Products
1901 Estes Ave.
Elk Grove Village IL 60007
847-427-0020
www.sculpey.com
manufacturer of Sculpey, Premo clays

Polymer Clay Express
9890 Main Street
Damascus MD 20872
800-844-0138
www.polymerclayexpress.com
on-line clay supplies,
Polymer Clay Express Clay Extruder

PolyPress
Kelly Dance
KellyLDance@aol.com
PolyPress Extruder

Poly-Tools, Inc
Gale and Sue Lee
PO Box 10
Woodson IL 62695
800-397-5201
www.poly-tools.com
tools

Prairie Craft Co.
PO Box 209
Florissant CO 80816
800-779-0615
www.prairiecraft.com
clay supplies, tools

Puffinalia
Linda Geer
PO Box 46211
Seattle WA 98146
www.puffinalia.com
miracle mold compound, supplies

Quilted in Clay
Jennifer Patterson
22924 - 450th Avenue N.W.
Alvarado MN 56710
218-965-4621
www.quiltedinclay.com
polymer clay quilt jewelry, extruder discs

Ready Stamps
10405 San Diego Mission Road, Ste. 103
San Diego CA 92108
619-282-8790
www.readystamps.com
custom rubber stamps

Rings & Things
PO Box 450
Spokane WA 99210
800-366-2156
www.rings-things
wholesale jewelry findings and beads

Rio Grande
7500 Bluewater Rd. NW
Albuquerque NM 87121
800-545-6566
www.riogrande.com
beads, gems, findings, supplies, tools,

Sarajane's
PO Box 263
Hygiene CO 80533-0263
www.polyclay.com
beads, buttons, wearable art, dolls, sculpture and more

Simply Darling Creations
Tamila Darling
www.simplydarling.com
Darlin' Designer Extruder Disks, minis and sets

Soft Flex
PO Box 80
Sonoma CA 95476
707-938-3539
www.softflextm.com
Softflex Wire, Artistic Wire

Wee Folks Creations
18476 Natchez Ave.
Prior Lake MN 55372
612-447-3828
www.weefolk.com
molds, classes, videos

ZigZag Polymer Clay Supplies
15 Pascoe Ave. St.
St. Albans Christchurch
New Zealand 8001
+64-3-385-4436
www.zigzag.co.nz
polymer clay, supplies, tools

12. References

Books – Polymer Clay

The Art of Jewelry Polymer Clay, Katherine Duncan Aimone, Lark Books, New York, NY, 2006

The Art of Polymer Clay, Donna Kato, Watson-Guptill Crafts, New York, NY, 2006

Artists At Work: Polymer Clay Comes of Age, Pierrette Brown Ashcroft, Lindly Haunani, Flower Valley Press, Rockville, MD, 1997

Celebrations with Polymer Clay, Sarajane Helm, Krause Publications, Iola, WI, 2003

Faux Surfaces in Polymer Clay: 30 Techniques & Projects That Imitate Stones, Metals, Wood & More, Irene Semanchuk Dean, Lark Books, New York, NY, 2005

Creating Life-Like Figures in Polymer Clay: A Step-By-Step Guide, Katherine Dewey, Elvenwork Press, 2003

Creating with Polymer Clay: Designs, Techniques, Projects, Stephen Ford, Leslie Dierks, Sterling, New York, NY, 1999

Creative Clay Jewelry: Extraordinary, Colorful, Fun Designs To Make From Polymer Clay, Leslie Dierks, Sterling, New York, NY, 1994

Creative Ways with Polymer Clay, Dotty McMillan, Sterling, New York, NY, 2002

Create a Polymer Clay Impression, Sarajane Helm, Krause Publications, Iola, WI, 2001

Foundations in Polymer Clay Design, Barbara A McGuire, Krause Publications, Iola, WI, 1999

Liquid Polymer Clay: Fabulous New Techniques for Making Jewelry and Home Accents, Ann Mitchell, Karen Mitchell, Krause Publications, Iola, WI, 2001

The New Clay, Nan Roche, Flower Valley Press, Rockville, MD, 1991

Polymer: The Chameleon Clay, Victoria Hughes, Krause Publications, Iola, WI, 2002

Polymer Clay Creative Traditions, Judy Belcher, Watson-Guptill Publications, New York, NY, 2006

Polymer Clay Creations: 11 Easy Projects You Can Make, Marie Segal, North Light Books, Cincinnati, OH, 2003

Polymer Clay Extravaganza, Lisa Pavelka, North Light Books, Cincinnati, OH, 2003

Polymer Clay for the First Time, syndee holt, Sterling, New York, NY, 2000

Polymer Clay Inspirations, Patricia Kimle, North Light Books, Cincinnati, OH, 2005

Polymer Clay Jewelry, Debbie Jackson, North Light Books, Cincinnati, OH, 2004

Polymer Clay Surface Design Recipes, Ellen Marshall, Quarry Books, Gloucester, MA, 2005

The Polymer Clay Techniques Book, Sue Heaser, North Light Books, Cincinnati, OH, 1999

Step by Step Polymer Clay in a Day: Over 15 Exciting Projects, from Gifts to Accessories for the Home, Emma Ralph North Light Books, Cincinnati, OH, 2003

The Weekend Crafter Polymer Clay, Irene Semanchuk Dean, Lark Books, Asheville, NC, 2000

Books – Quilts & Textiles

501 Quilt Blocks, Lewis & Childs, Better Homes and Gardens Books, Des Moines, IA, 1994

An Amish Adventure, Roberta Horton, C&T Publishing, Lafayette, CA, 1996

The Amish Quilt, Eve Wheatcroft Granick, Good Books, Intercourse, PA, 1989

America's Traditional Crafts, Robert Shaw, Hugh Lauter Levin Associates, Inc., Westport, CT, 1993

Art and Inspirations, Michael James, C&T Publishing, Lafayette, CA, 1998

The Art Quilt, Robert Shaw, Hugh Lauter Levin Associates, Inc., Westport, CT, 1997

The Big Book of Small Quilts, Mary Hickey, Oxmoor House, Inc., Birmingham, AL, 1997

Curves in Motion, Judy B. Dales, C&T Publishing, Lafayette, CA, 1998

Designing Tessellations, Jinny Beyer, Contemporary Books, Lincolnwood, IL, 1999

A Gallery of Amish Quilts, Robert Bishop & Elizabeth Safanda, E P Dutton & Co., New York, NY, 1976

Kaleidoscopes and Quilts, Paula Nadelstern, C&T Publishing, Lafayette, CA, 1996

Mariner's Compass Quilts, Judy Mathieson, C&T Publishing, Lafayette, CA, 1993

The New Sampler Quilt, Diana Leone, C&T Publishing, Lafayette, CA, 1993

A People and Their Quilts, John Rice Irwin, Schiffer Publishing Ltd, Atglen, PA, 1984

Quilting Among Friends, Jill Reber, Landauer Books, Urbandale, IA, 2005

Quilts in the Tradition of Frank Lloyd Wright, Jackie Robinson, Animas Quilts Publishing, Durango, CO, 1995

Quilting Masterclass, Katharine Guerrier, That Patchwork Place, Bothell, WA, 2000

Quilts of Illusion, Laura Fisher, Sterling Publishing Co., New York, NY, 1990

Tessellations, Jackie Robinson, Animas Quilts Publishing, Eureka, MT, 1992

Textile Designs, Susan Meller and Joost Elffers, Harry N. Abrams, Inc., New York, NY, 2002

A Treasury of Mennonite Quilte, Rachel and Kenneth Pellman, Good Books, Intercourse, PA, 1992

The Ultimate Quilting Book, Maggi McCormick Gordon, Sterling Publishing Co, New York, NY, 2001

The World of Amish Quilts, Rachel and Kenneth Pellman, Good Books, Intercourse, PA, 1984

Books – Color

Blue and Yellow Don't Make Green, Michael Wilcox, North Light Books, Cincinnati, OH, 1987

Color, A Natural History of the Palette, Victoria Finley, Random House Trade Paperbacks, New York, 2002

Color Magic for Quilters, Ann Seely & Joyce Stewart, Rodale Quilt Book, Emmaus, PA, 1997

Dyeing to Quilt, Joyce Mori and Cynthia Myerberg, The Quilt Digest Press, Lincolnwood, IL, 1997

Jinny Beyer's Color Confidence for Quilters, McGraw-Hill; 1 edition (January 11, 1992)

The Elements of Color, Johannes Itten, Van Nostrand Reinhold Company, New York, NY, 1970

Hand Dyed Fabric Made Easy, Adriene Buffington, That Patchwork Place, Bothell, WA, 1996

Interaction of Color, Josef Albers, Yale University Press, New Haven and London, 1971

Magazines

Art Jewelry
Kalmbach Publishing
PO Box 1612
Waukesha WI 53187
800-533-6644
www.artjewelrymag.com

Belle Armoire
22992 Mill Creek, Ste. B
Laguna Hills CA 92653
877-STAMPER
www.bellearmoire.com

Bead & Button
Kalmbach Publishing
PO Box 1612
Waukesha WI 53187
800-533-6644
www.beadandbutton.com

The Crafts Report
300 Water St.
Wilmington DE 19801
www.craftsreport.com

Fiberarts Magazine
Nine Press, 50 College St.
Asheville NC 28801
704-253-0467
www.larkbooks.com

Fiber Studio Press
20205 144th Ave. NE
Woodenville WA 98072
800-426-3126
www.patchwork.com

Interweave Press
201 E. Fourth St.
Loveland CO 80537
800-645-3675
www.interweave.com

PolymerCafe
30595 Eight Mile Rd
Livonia MI 48152
800-458-8237
www.polymercafe.com

Ornament Magazine
PO Box 2349
San Marcos CA 92079
800-888-8950
ornamentmagazine.com

Somerset Studio
22992 Mill Creek, Ste. B
Laguna Hills CA 92653
877-STAMPER
www.somersetstudio.com

Threads Magazine
63 S. Main St.
Newtown CT 06470
800-888-8286
www.taunton.com

PolyMarket Press
PO Box 263
Hygiene CO 80533-0263
www.PolyMarketPress.com
books, print media

Websites

Bead Bugle
www.beadbugle.com
online magazine

Colours In Clay
Elaine Robitaille
www.tooaquarius.com/learn/colours
colour mixing charts

Glass Attic
www.glassattic.com
polymer clay information archive

National Polymer Clay Guild
PMB 345 1350 Beverly Rd., 115
McClean VA 22101
www.npcg.org
polymer clay organization

Plastics Historical Society
www.plastiquarian.com/ind1.htm
history and composition of plastics

Polymer Clay Central
www.polymerclaycentral.com
information and forum on polymer clay

Polymer Clay Daily
www.polymerclaydaily.com
polymer clay artists gallery

photo: Jim Doane

13. Glossary

With thanks to Nan Roche, Barbara McGuire and Merriam-Webster.

Achromatic - Free from color

Acrylic - Derived from acrylic acid or acrylonitrile; containing acrylic resin Plexiglass is an acrylic thermoplastic and is used in sheets for work surfaces, rods for clay rollers

Analogous colors - A group of colors that lie side by side on the color wheel

Appliqué - To apply on top of

Armature - A skeleton or framework on which clay pieces are built to give support and reduce the amount of clay volume inside. Paper, wire, aluminum foil are some items used.

Brayer - Roller tool with a handle

Buffing wheel - Machine driving wheel with a muslin or flannel disc for bringing polymer to a shine

Bulls-eye - A cane design in circles that increase in size and radiate out from a midpoint, like a target

Cane - A term borrowed from glass working that refers to patterned or solid colored rods placed to form a design. Slices of canes are used to create millefiore work.

Chroma - The purity of a color or its freedom from white or gray

Clay - A fine suspension of aluminum silicate, moldable when wet and fused into permanent form at very high temperatures

Clay Block - A small unit of polymer clay, usually 2 or 3 ounces

Clay Brick - A large unit of polymer clay, usually 13 to 16 ounces

Conditioning - Preparation of clay before use to warm and soften it and align molecules for permanent strength

Convection oven - Oven with a continuous flow of air that keeps temperatures even throughout

Cure - The process of hardening polymer clay with heat

Cut-outs - Shapes made using cookie cutters or similar tools

Cutters - Any shaped metal tool that cuts repeatable designs, from small Kemper cutters to cookie cutters

Discs - Round die made of acrylic or metal with shaped openings for use with extruders

Diluent - Liquid plasticiser to soften hard clays

Embossing powder - Particles used in stamping designs or as inclusions that react with heat to expand and become glossy

Extrusions - Shaped lengths of clay made using a tool that presses soft clay out through a disc (die) with a precisely cut opening

Forms - Shapes on which clay can be baked

Findings - The mechanical parts of jewelry making; clasps, pin backs, earring parts and more

Finish - Any way of smoothing the surface or giving a shine including sanding and buffing, or added glosses and glazes. Compatable products include those made by polymer clay manufacturers, Future Acrylic Floor Polish™, Rust-Oleum Waterbased Varathane™

Glass - A hard, brittle, transparent, noncrystaline substance produced by fusion of silicates containing soda and lime at very high temperatures

Grit - Degree of coarseness in sandpaper or powders; low numbers such as 60 are very coarse and range to superfine automotive grade at 1200 and 2000

Guild - Group of individuals who come together for a common purpose; the National Polymer Clay Guild and local guilds are a great way to share and exchange information and experiences

Hue - The color of an object; classed as red, blue, green, or yellow in reference to the spectrum

Inclusions - Powders or other materials such as glitter, fibers or spices that are put into the body of the clay, affecting color and texture

Jellyroll - Spiral cane made with two colors rolled up and sliced like a cinnamon bun

Loaves - Square or rectangular clay assemblies; sometimes sliced from the top as in Mokume Gane

Log - Cane component like a snake but thicker, also sometimes refers to canes

Marbelize - The incomplete mixing of two or more colors that creates the appearance of marble or stone

Mica Powders - Shiny pigmented powders that contain mica and give the look of metal or shell, or that have interference qualities affecting the perceived color. Can be used on top or inside clays

Millefiore - Literally Italian for 'thousand flowers'; refers to glass making technique that uses patterned and colored rods of glass to form canes, slices of which decorate objects like beads and paper weights.

Mokume Gane - A Japanese metal working technique adapted to polymer that uses clay sheets stacked and layered with metallic foils to form loaves. Areas are raised or lowered with impressions from top or bottom and a blade is used to slice thin pieces horizontally from the top

Molds - A negative relief impression that allow replication using clay pressed in and pulled out; can be made using polymer clay or silicone compounds, metal, acrylics, glass or plaster of paris

Monochromatic - Colors made from tints or shades of the same hue

Morphing - The process of changing a component from one shape to another. It can also be done to a square cane to change the corners into the flat parts and the flat parts into corners.

Onlay - The application of a layer of clay onto another layer of clay

Opaque - Neither reflecting or emitting light, not transparent or translucent

Parchment Paper - An oven baking paper useful for eliminating shiny spots on polymer clay, also useful as a work surface liner

Pasta Machine - Roller device designed for making noodles, and used with polymer clay to condition, blend colors, texturize and create even sheets of clay of 7-9 variable thicknesses. Comes with hand crank and removable noodle cutters that will cut raw or cured into strips. A motor is also available.

Pearlescent - Shimmering clay that contains small mica particles and reflects light. Used in mica-shift techniques to create a raised image visible inside the flat surface of the clay

Photocopy Transfer - Technique that uses the plasticisers in polymer clays to transfer ink from photocopied images onto the clay. Liquid clays form soft peel-off sheets that contain the image after baking and can be appliquéd and re-baked.

Pigment - Coloring agent

Plastic - Literally "changeable"; refers to any natural and synthetic materials that can be shaped when soft and then hardened. Includes resins such as amber, resinoids, polymers, cellulose derivatives (like celluloid) casein materials and protein

Plasticiser - Any of a group of organic substances used in plastics to impart viscosity, flexibility, softness, and other qualities

Polymer - A very large molecule made up of many smaller units joined together, generally end to end, to create a long chain. The smallest "building block" of a polymer is called a monomer (mono = one)

Polymer Clay - A modern modeling compound composed primarily of PVC resin, plasticiser, and pigments as well as other fillers including mica

Polyvinyl chloride - Known as PVC; a white, water insoluable, thermoplastic resin used in making record albums, plumbing pipes and polymer clays

Plugs - Short fat rolls of clay, often sliced into and added to before reduction into snakes

Pulver - Powders made of powdered aluminum and pigment. Use with a air mask

Reduction - Squeezing and compressing the cane in on itself as the cane is also stretched to lengthen it causes the scale of the design to become smaller. This can be done a little or a lot

Release agent - Powder, cornstarch or misted water used on molds or stamps to allow clay to be pulled away after impression

Saturation - The degree of chroma or purity of color; the degree of freedom from mixture with white

Shade - The degree of darkness of a color determined by the quantity of black added

Sheets - Flat, even layers of clay made by rolling the clay with an acrylic rod, a brayer, or a pasta machine

Skinner Blend - Technique allowing the even gradient blending of two or more colors of clay, developed by Judith Skinner

Slamming - Forcefully throwing the cane down on a flat surface to help "wake up" canes that are slow to move. Also refers to the process of putting canes together quickly or within a group caning process

Snakes - Rolled out pieces of clay that are long with a round diameter Also referred to by other shapes as in triangle, teardrop or square snakes

Spiral - Curled image inside a cane made by rolling up two colored sheets in a jellyroll fashion

Stamp - Texture tool with a positive or raised image that allows the design to be impressed into the surface of clay or used with inks or embossing agents to pattern the surface

Strips - Clay pieces not as wide as tongues that can easily be formed by flattening a snake of clay by pressing with your thumb or a roller to flatten onto the work surface

Tessellations – Designs that interlock to repeat across a surface

Thermoplastics - Polymers that once formed can be heated and reformed over and over again

Thermosets - Polymers that are formed and then heat cured into a permanent shape

Tint - A color diluted with white

Tongues - Sheets of clay, formed by hand, that are longer than they are wide, and thicker than a rolled sheet

Translucent - Admitting or diffusing light so objects can not be seen clearly through it. Refers also to clay with no pigments or fillers that can be sliced very thin and buffed almost clear

Transparent - Transmitting of light so objects can be seen clearly through it

Value - Degree of lightness or darkness of a color

Varathane™ - Line of wood finishing products made by Rust-Oleum; the water based indoor version is compatible with polymer clay as is the water based spray

Wedges - Components shaped like triangle snakes but are cut at an angle from sheets of stacked clay

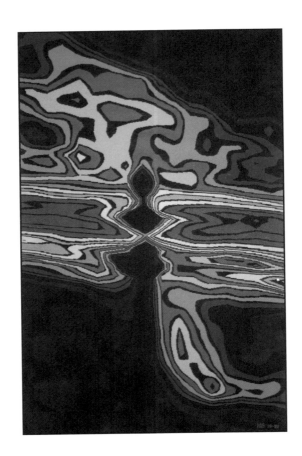

Judith Skinner is living her dream in a log cabin in a mountain town in Arizona.

She lives with three dogs, two cats and polymer clay everywhere. Her work is featured in local cooperative art galleries in Prescott and Jerome. She leads workshops locally and with guilds around the country.

Judith is best known around the world as the originator of the "Skinner Blend", a gradient color mixing technique used by polymer clay artists everywhere.

Her background in sewing, needlework, software design and polymer clay all contributed to the variety of skills used in creating this book.

Visit her websites:
www.judithskinner.com

www.artsprescott.com
www.jeromeartistscoop.com

Sarajane Helm has been making things all her life and loves it still. Beads, masks, miniatures and dolls all find their way out of her workrooms in the foothills of the Rocky Mountains.

She lives with her husband and sons. They all enjoy the many uses of polymer clay right along with her as they live amidst the many projects.

Sarajane's previous books include *Create A Polymer Clay Impression* and *Celebrations With Polymer Clay* (Krause Publications).

In addition to other magazine articles and web design, she writes a Professional Arts column for *Belle Armoire* magazine and a column about polymer clay for the online BeadBugle.com

Visit her websites:
www.polyclay.com

www.beadlounge.com
www.polymarketpress.com